Conquering Debt

God's Way

Bruce Ammons

with

Ruthie Ammons

Find freedom from your enemy...

Here's what people are saying about *Conquering Debt God's Way* seminars:

> "*Excellent job! Your presentation is informational, inspiring, and challenging. You do a good job.... I believe you share some of the best principles that I have read or heard on the subject.*"

❖

> "*Words cannot express what we as a church feel after the tremendous* Conquering Debt God's Way *seminar. People were changed in such numerous ways.... Thank you for being obedient to God's call on your life. It's obvious He has blessed and will continue to bless your very needed and highly effective ministry.*"

❖

> "*We had been praying all summer for an answer to paying for the kids' Christian college education, and you were the answer to that prayer. God bless you in your ministry.*"

❖

> "*Your seminar and your book have been life-changing! We've completely changed our ways of finance, tithing, paying off debts, and most importantly — our relationship with God and with each other.... Our marriage has made a complete 180° turn and God is blessing it every day — he's given us a joy that we had never felt before.*"

"Since taking your seminar, we have eliminated $48,000 in debt over the first 15 months, and now we are working to pay off our home loans, add to savings, and for the first time ever, give over and above our tithe in offerings. We have also received thousands in surprise money from God."

"Bruce conducted his seminar for our congregation…and some families who attended this seminar have freed themselves from all debt. One of our families has not only tripled their weekly contribution, they have reduced their debt by fifty-thousand dollars in only 8 months. No, they did not get another job or a pay raise. They simply applied the biblical principles taught in this seminar."

"The principles you taught us…have been life changing and we have seen God's faithfulness to us in unbelievable ways over this past year…. Over 50% of our budget was committed to minimum monthly debt payments. In one year, we have eliminated almost $20,000 in debt! All Christians have points in their lives where they can look back and see that God was spurring them on to a deeper walk with Him. For us, Conquering Debt God's Way *is one of those points…."*

Conquering Debt | God's Way

BRUCE AMMONS with **RUTHIE AMMONS**

Conquering Debt God's Way

HillCrest
PUBLISHING

1648 Campus Court
Abilene, TX 79601
www.hillcrestpublishing.com

**Copyright © 2003
Bruce Ammons**

This book is set in ITC Giovanni 11/14 with titling in Helvetica Neue. This book was composed in Adobe InDesign.

ISBN 0–89112–491–8

LCCN 2002114029

¶ 5 4 3 2 1

Dedication

To our parents,
  Darryl & Dot Ammons and Jerry & Mary Anne Fortune:
  It was an honor to grow up in your homes. It was there that we
  received training in biblical principles of living. And we still turn
  to you for unconditional love, intimate friendship, prayer support,
  and wise counsel. Eat right and exercise. We need you around for
  a long time!

To John Maxwell and Rick Warren:
  Though I have never even met you, I've been discipled by you both
  through your cassette tape ministries. I'd be frightened to know how
  much money I've spent on your resources—but it was some of the
  best money I've ever spent. God has used you to shape, mold, inspire,
  educate, motivate, convict, and change me. Recurring themes from
  your ministries are likely found throughout this book; I cannot escape
  them. I hope to meet you both someday (and let's throw in a round
  of golf while we're at it)!

Disclaimer

It is not the intent of this book or its authors to provide professional tax, investment, or legal counsel. Please consult an attorney, accountant, financial planner, or other professional for these services.

Every effort has been made to make this book as complete and accurate as possible. However, there may be mistakes, both in book production and in book content. Therefore, this text should be used only as a general guideline and not as the ultimate source of financial information. A few stories have been slightly altered to protect the identity of those involved. However, great care has been taken to be true to the biblical principles illustrated by these stories.

The purpose of this book is to *educate* and *motivate*. The author and HillCrest Publishing shall have neither liability nor responsibility to any person or entity with respect to any loss or damage caused, or alleged to be caused, directly or indirectly, by the information contained in this book.

Contents

Symbol Key

This book uses several symbols to highlight key points and to mark helpful information. Look for them in the margins as you read. Here's a brief introduction:

Scriptural backgrounds and discussion

Surprising facts

Helpful tips and tricks

Hints about money and budgeting

Reader worksheets and interactive information

preface

The Cycle of Debt

Did you realize that the average baby born in the United States of America is literally born into debt?

Let me explain what I mean by that. Imagine a young married couple who are expecting their first baby. They're filled with excitement as they anticipate the birth of this little bundle of joy. When the due time arrives, they rush off to the hospital. They give birth, and all their dreams have come true.

Please notice what happens next. Most couples cannot afford to pay this baby off when it's time to leave the hospital, so they have to make arrangements to pay this baby off in monthly payments. This baby has literally been born into debt.

Then these new parents take this newborn and place it carefully into an automobile that they're paying off on a five-year loan, and drive it across town to a house they're paying off on a thirty-year mortgage.

As this child begins to grow up in this home, several things will become commonplace. It will be the norm for this child to sleep on "mortgaged" beds, sit on "mortgaged" furniture, watch a "mortgaged" television, wear "mortgaged" clothes, and do homework on a "mortgaged" computer (even though there are no payments or interest due for the next six months).

When this child turns 18 and decides to go to college, how do you think his family will fund his college education? A Student Education Loan, naturally. While at college, this young man will fall in love with a young lady and ask her to marry him. She says yes. They'll go shopping for an engagement ring. How do you think they'll pay for this ring? A credit card (or another type of loan).

This couple gets married, goes on a honeymoon (often on credit), returns home, completes college, and then gets jobs. Now this young couple has income that qualifies them for all types of credit purchasing. They decide to purchase a couple of new automobiles and place them on five-year payment plans. Then they decide they don't want to throw their money away by paying rent, so they "purchase" a home on a thirty-year mortgage.

Shortly thereafter, they turn up expecting a baby. They're so excited—they can hardly wait until the day comes when they give birth to their little bundle of joy. When the due time arrives, they rush off to the hospital, give birth to a precious baby, but of course cannot pay off the little one when it's time to check out of the hospital. So they work out a convenient monthly payment plan with the hospital in order to "get this child paid off."

This describes the vicious cycle that most Americans are caught up in. In fact, most of us are not only born into debt, but we never get completely out of debt until we die. What a *terrible* way to live. I can assure you that when Jesus Christ promised us abundant life, he was not talking about a lifestyle like the one described above.

Yet this lifestyle is so commonplace even among Christians. Debt is the American way. It's the normal lifestyle in this country. Most of us live our lives thinking in terms of monthly payments. If you are considering the purchase of a new big screen television, you probably don't ask yourself if you can afford $1999. Rather, you ask yourself if you can afford $58 per month. If you're looking to buy a new automobile, you probably don't ask yourself if you can afford $27,000. Rather, you ask yourself if you can afford $399.99 per month. Such is life in the good old USA...

Sick and Tired of Being Sick and Tired!

One day I awoke extremely tired of the lifestyle that I have just described to you. I was sick and tired of the debt-plagued life. I felt a lot like a rubber band that was stretched to its limit and was about to break at any moment.

I was sick and tired of the stress, and the burden, and the pressure of having more month than money. I was sick and tired of arguing with my lovely wife Ruthie about money problems.

I was sick and tired of the late payment notices that regularly came from my credit card companies (along with added fees. I have yet to discover how a credit card company comes to the conclusion that I can afford the extra fees when I can't even afford the minimum payment). I was sick and tired of the insufficient funds notices that came from my bank (along with *more* extra fees). I was sick and tired of being harassed on the telephone from my many disgruntled creditors.

I was sick and tired of the anxiety that I felt 24 hours a day, 7 days per week, 365 days per year.

I was sick and tired of being unable to get a good night's sleep because of constant financial worries.

I was sick and tired of the relationship difficulties this debt and resulting stress brought into my extended family. A relative loaned us some money to help us, and then we were unable to repay the relative as we had promised—do you know the definition of a distant relative? I do. When you're unable to repay a loan to a relative, it creates a distance that is incredibly unhealthy and uncomfortable. I found myself wanting to skip family reunions because I was embarrassed to see this relative. (Thanks to the concepts taught in this book, we have now paid off this relative and all is well again).

I was sick and tired of our inability to enjoy a family vacation. I remember taking my wife Ruthie and daughter Carlee (before the birth of two more precious daughters, Shaylee and Allee) to an amusement park in Dallas, Texas. Carlee and I were riding a ride called the Parachute. As we were descending, I looked at Carlee and she was clearly having the time of her life. Her eyes were big, and her mouth was open wide as she gasped with enthusiasm. As I realized the great joy she was experiencing, I became overwhelmed because I wasn't experiencing the same joy. In fact, I was miserable. As I considered the source of my misery, I realized that I was worried about how we were going to pay for this trip once we returned home. I knew that I had put the gasoline for the automobile, the food we were eating, the motel at which we were staying, and the amusement park tickets on a credit card. On top of all this, we were already in financial trouble *before* we left home. My financial debt had literally stolen the enjoyment out of this vacation for me.

I was sick and tired of giving less than my best at my job. God has called me into the gospel ministry. But I was unable to give my best to my congregation, the lost community, and to my God because I was so preoccupied with financial problems that I was unable to focus my energies effectively on glorifying my Lord through my vocation.

I was sick and tired of giving less than my best at home. I was not the kind of husband or father that God had called me to be, due to my preoccupation with financial problems.

I was sick and tired of withholding my "tithe" from the Lord. As a minister of the gospel of Jesus Christ, I received my living from the tithes and offerings of God's people. Yet, I was not tithing and giving offerings as the Lord had commanded. I wanted to tithe, but I simply couldn't figure out a way to do so, due to our financial predicament.

Due to living under such pressure for twelve consecutive years, on October 22, a few years ago, I had an emotional breakdown. My emotional rubber band broke. But Ruthie and I did something on that day that forever changed our lives.

As a result, 5 months later, we were completely debt-free (excluding our mortgage). This was a huge accomplishment, as our debt load was at an all-time high. We had attempted to pay off our debts for twelve years without any success. Suddenly, we had accomplished something in just 5 *months* that we were previously unable to accomplish in twelve *years* of miserable labor.

We have since been able to pay off a thirty-year mortgage in less than 5 years. This book will reveal five different strategies that show how to pay off a thirty-year mortgage in 5 years or less. If you use several strategies at once, you may be able to pay off your mortgage even faster. We know of one family that paid off every debt to their name (including house and cars) in only 8 months, using the exciting strategies found in this book. Another family did so in 11 months, and another in 14 months. However, it is only fair for you to know that these examples are not the norm. For the average American, it typically takes approximately 5 years to pay off *all* debt (including house and cars) by following the strategies I will teach you in this book.

Please don't give in to the temptation to skip ahead. As you'll soon see, the principles are intentionally built in a certain order. Applying the principles in the proper order is one of the keys to success.

introduction

The Biblical Strategy

The "Conquering Debt God's Way" strategy is built upon principles from the book of Joshua. We'll focus primarily on chapters 10 and 11. But before looking at the text, we need to understand the context of this passage of Scripture.

This is not a story about finances. This is a story of God leading his people from the land of bondage to the land of blessing. It's a story of how God brought his people from slavery in Egypt, where they had been in bondage for 400 years, into the Promised Land.

One day as Ruthie and I considered this story, we began to ask ourselves if this same God who delivered his children into the land of blessing could do a similar miracle with us in relation to our finances. In other words, we were trapped in the land of financial bondage and needed deliverance into the land of financial blessing.

As we read the biblical account, we began searching for the universal principles that God used for deliverance. Five principles came to the surface. We determined to apply these same principles to our finances, and to our amazement we saw our financial debt defeated right before our eyes.

Since then, we've taught these principles to thousands through the live "Conquering Debt God's Way" seminar (for information about hosting a live seminar, go to www.conqueringdebt.com). They have experienced the wonderful work of God in their financial lives as well. Many have now successfully eliminated their entire financial debt, including house and cars.

But let me hasten to share with you that these same principles apply to other areas of our lives as well. One day I got a call from a lady who had attended the seminar. She was ecstatic. She shared that she had eliminated a lot of debt as a result of diligently applying the principles, but that she was most excited about all the weight she had lost. She went on to share that she had been 40 pounds overweight for years but had lost all 40 pounds and had kept it off. I asked her what the seminar had to do with her weight loss. She reminded me of the five principles found in Joshua in which God delivered his people from bondage to blessing. She went on to share how she had applied the same principles to her bondage to overeating. God delivered her—and she has lost the weight for good.

God can bring you out of bondage to more than just debt...

I found this fascinating, especially since I was 30 pounds overweight at the time. I decided to use these same steps in addressing my overweight problem and have since lost the 30 pounds—and kept it off.

Another seminar attendee called and reported breaking his addiction to smoking cigarettes (2 packs per day for 10 years). He hasn't touched another cigarette since the seminar! He simply applied the same principles to his tobacco bondage.

It's time to get excited! Let's get to the text, discover the principles, apply them diligently, and conquer debt God's way!

The Main Text: Joshua 10:5–14 (NASV)

5 *So the five kings of the Amorites, the king of Jerusalem, the king of Hebron, the king of Jarmuth, the king of Lachish, and the king of Eglon, gathered together and went up, they with all their armies, and camped by Gibeon and fought against it.*

6   *Then the men of Gibeon sent word to Joshua to the camp at Gilgal saying, "Do not abandon your servants; come up to us quickly and save us and help us, for all the kings of the Amorites that live in the hill country have assembled against us."*

7   *So Joshua went up from Gilgal, he and all the people of war with him and all the valiant warriors.*

8   *The LORD said to Joshua, "Do not fear them, for I have given them into your hands; not one of them shall stand before you."*

9   *So Joshua came upon them suddenly by marching all night from Gilgal.*

10   *And the LORD confounded them before Israel, and He slew them with a great slaughter at Gibeon, and pursued them by way of ascent of Beth-Horon and struck them as far as Azekah and Makkedah.*

11   *And it came about as they fled from before Israel, while they were at the descent of Beth-Horon, the LORD threw large stones from heaven on them as far as Azekah, and they died; there were more who died from the hailstones than those whom the sons of Israel killed with the sword.*

12   *Then Joshua spoke to the LORD in the day when the LORD delivered up the Amorites before the sons of Israel, and he said in the sight of Israel, "O sun, stand still at Gibeon, and O moon in the valley of Aijalon."*

13   *So the sun stood still, and the moon stopped, until the nation avenged themselves of their enemies. Is it not written in the book of Jashar? And the sun stopped in the middle of the sky and did not hasten to go down for about a whole day.*

14   *There was no day like that before it or after it, when the LORD listened to the voice of a man; for the LORD fought for Israel.*

Principle 1: Joshua Defined His Enemy

We are introduced to Joshua's enemy in verse 5 — the Amorites. In order to get a more complete understanding of God's command, we would need to go back to the book of Deuteronomy. To make a long story short, God commanded Joshua to kill *all* the Amorites. God emphasized his order by saying that when this military campaign was complete, there should not be a single Amorite left breathing. God's call was clear—complete annihilation of the Amorite people group.

Joshua knew what God required of him—a series of military strikes that would take several years of intensive warfare. The job was a big one and a tough one. And, it could be accomplished only with God's help .

Just as Joshua was clear about who his enemy was, we must come to clarity about our financial enemy. I would like to submit to you that debt is your enemy; it is *not* your friend!

Many believe that debt *is* their friend, though. The thinking goes like this: "I could not have this house if it were not for debt; debt must be my friend. I could not have this car if it were not for debt; debt must be my friend."

I can assure you that you cannot eliminate debt if you think it's your friend. You have to come to the clear con-

Debt is your enemy — as serious as any enemy faced by God's people…

clusion that debt is *your enemy*, or you will likely remain enslaved to it for all your days. When we go into detail in Step 1, I'll give you five solid proofs that debt is your enemy.

Principle 2: Joshua Declared War Against His Enemy

In verse 9, we find Joshua and his army involved in a 25-mile, all-night march from Gilgal to Gibeon. This action illustrated their *commitment* to conquer the enemy. Joshua and his army were saying to themselves and to God that they were serious. They were committed. They were not playing games. They were willing to get out of their La-Z-Boy™ recliners and turn off the cable television to go into a hostile land to fight their enemy. Joshua was saying that he was willing to obey God no matter what the cost.

In like fashion, we must come to the place where we are intensely committed to conquering debt. We must stop playing games and become serious about debt elimination.

I remember the day I told Ruthie that I was sick and tired of living under the intense pressure of debt. I expressed the fact that I was so frustrated with life as we were experiencing it that I was willing to do *anything* that God called me to do to eliminate debt—regardless of the cost. I realized the cost might be great. But just as Joshua was willing to go to war even if it cost him his life, I was willing to go to war against debt even if it cost me my life.

Ruthie agreed with me and made the same commitment, and the war was on!

For those of you who are married, it is important to realize that it takes both of you to be committed to this war. If only one spouse enters this war, failure and marital struggles are guaranteed. But, if you both commit to the process, success will follow—along with a fresh drawing together in your marital relationship.

> Conquering the enemy—debt—will make you and your spouse closer allies!

Principle 3: Joshua Demonstrated Fearless Faith

I define faith as "God speaks; I obey, whether what God says makes sense or not." Joshua demonstrated faith beautifully in chapter six where we read of the conquest of Jericho. Remember the story?

One day Joshua and his army came upon a city known as Jericho. Joshua noticed that the city was surrounded with tall walls. Joshua asked God, "How are we going to climb over those walls?" God replied, "You're not going to climb those walls." Joshua asked, "What shall we do then, take our bows and arrows and shoot stray arrows over the wall and hope the arrows find the hearts of our enemies?" God said, "You're not going to need your bows and arrows. In fact, drop your weapons. Instead of weapons, pick up trumpets, and march around those walls while playing some pretty music."

This was one of the most unusual battle strategies of all times. What Joshua really needed was weapons—machine guns or Apache helicopters, maybe. But, God told him to drop the very thing he needed most—weapons.

This battle strategy of course made no sense to Joshua. Yet Joshua basically said, "God, I trust you so much that I will obey you, even though your command makes no sense to my human, finite mind." What a wonderful picture of fearless faith! God was actually testing Joshua—and Joshua passed the test. As a result, God knocked down the walls of Jericho and led Joshua to a swift and miraculous victory. This victory was over a much bigger and stronger army. Yet, the size of the enemy doesn't matter when you have God on your side. Just ask David (of Goliath-slaying fame).

It's important to consider what would have occurred had Joshua decided to disobey. We don't even have to speculate to discover the answer. Simply turn to Joshua 7 and read about Joshua's own defeat at Ai. Due to disobedience in the camp (on the part of Achan), God allowed a much weaker army to defeat Joshua's army. In these back-to-back chapters, we discover that God will do miracles to help his people when they are obedient; yet he will actually help the enemy when his people are disobedient.

When it comes to debt elimination, God also issues us a faith test. He wants to see if you really trust him or if you're just playing a game. God will literally ask you to do some things that make *no sense* to your human, finite mind. He'll ask you to do some things that are the *exact opposite* of what the world teaches about debt elimination. At that moment, you'll have a choice to make—trust God or go with what makes the most sense to you. For those who

God's strategies for conquering debt may test your faith...

really trust him as Joshua did, the rewards are great. He will come through and knock down the walls of your debt for you. For those who choose to go with their own plan as Achan did, negative consequences are guaranteed!

Principle 4: Joshua Was Disciplined In His Efforts

If you take the time to read the entire book of Joshua, you will see that Joshua was highly disciplined in all that God called him to do.

The Bible is full of verses that teach the virtues of self-discipline. Some of my favorites include:

> *For God did not give us the spirit of fear, but a spirit of power, of love, and of self-discipline.* 2 Timothy 1:7

> *The fruit of the Spirit is love, joy, peace, patience, kindness, goodness, faithfulness, gentleness, and self-control.* Galatians 5:22–23

You may be thinking, "Oh no, I've never had self-discipline in my life." I have great news for you. I had never been a self-disciplined person before that fateful October 22, a few years ago, either. But God taught me how to become self-disciplined in no time at all. I'll explain later the tool God used to teach me discipline so rapidly.

Make no mistake about it. There are some things you have to do in a very disciplined way in order to become debt-free. Don't let this discourage you. After all is said and done, one of your greatest rewards of this entire battle will be the reward of self-discipline, benefiting you in many ways for years to come.

Principle 5: Joshua Looked To God For Divine Intervention

In Joshua 10:12–13, we see God doing miracles to help Joshua kill the enemies God told him to kill. Verse 12 indicates that God killed more of the enemies by miracle than Joshua and his army killed by sword.

How would you like for God to help you kill your enemy of debt? He *wants* to help you. One of my favorite illustrations in Scripture is when Peter approached Jesus one day with a financial concern. He reminded Jesus that they both owed money for taxes, yet neither had any money.

This would be similar to you or me owing the Internal Revenue Service some money, yet having none. When Peter talked with Jesus about the issue, Jesus determined that they needed some "miracle money." He told Peter to go fishing. When Peter caught a fish, he was to open the mouth of the fish where he would find a gold coin worth enough to pay off both their taxes. Of course, this literally happened (Matthew 17:24–27). God did a financial miracle to solve a financial problem.

I don't know whether you like to fish or not, but I have some exciting news for you. God may choose to pay off every debt to your name through the mouth of a fish. I'm not kidding!

While God did not pay off our debt through the mouth of a fish, he did do miracle after miracle to help us in our war on debt. During the 5 months following our commitment, God brought us 48 separate occasions of "miracle money" to assist us. And God has continued to help us many times since.

We hear many stories of people — just like you — who decided to follow the strategies set forth in this book. They share how God has canceled some of their financial debts by miracle and brought surprise money and other miracles into their lives to help them expedite the debt-elimination process.

The ABCs of God's Intervention

Ask God to help you.
Believe that God will help you.
Continue paying off debt with a passion!

Recently, an elder of a church informed me that he had paid off over $50,000 of debt in only 8 months by following the strategies outlined in this book. He was so excited to report that over $11,000 of it came as "miracle money" from the Lord.

As he did for Joshua, God will help you to conquer the very enemy he has commanded you to conquer.

chapter **1**

Define Your Enemy

I've become absolutely convinced that debt is our enemy;
it is not our friend! I'd like to illustrate this statement
with the following examples:

Mortgage

If you have a $100,000 mortgage and pay it out over a
thirty-year period, you will pay approximately $300,000
for that house. Not a good deal! Please notice the mystery
of the missing $200,000. Where did it go? It was thrown
away in interest.

Let me ask you two questions about this $200,000. Who
earned this money—you or the mortgage company? Answer:
you did! Who gets this money? Answer: they do!

This makes me angry. It disturbs me to think that I will
have to spend thirty years of my life earning $200,000 so
that I can throw it away in interest payments.

I'll have to spend my time, talents, energy, abilities, sweat,
and possibly blood and tears to produce this kind of income.
I'll spend time away from my family and friends in order
to produce this income. I may even be spending time away
from God to earn this money. I may not be able to volunteer
large amounts of my time for service or ministry projects
since my time is already spoken for—I must use it to produce
an income so I can earn $200,000 so I can throw it away in
interest payments. Indeed "the borrower is a slave to the
lender" (Proverbs 22:7).

I'll show you how to put a large portion of this $200,000 back into your own pocket for things such as vehicle replacements, college education, retirement needs, emergency reserve, and extra giving to the kingdom of God. Think about it. We're going to find a *way* to take the same money that you *already earn* and direct it away from interest payments and toward other more important life goals. This is indeed exciting and is worthy of our time and efforts!

You may be wondering if I believe that people should save up cash in order to purchase their first home. Absolutely not! I believe that people should borrow money for the purchase of their first home if necessary. However, I think it's wise to buy half the house you qualify for and double the monthly payments.

By following this formula, you'll transform a thirty-year mortgage into a much shorter-term mortgage. Though it seems like this would reduce the mortgage to fifteen years, it actually takes it down to around five years (it only takes about $100 extra per month to take a mortgage from thirty years to fifteen years for most of us).

 An extra payment of as little as $100 per month can turn a 30-year mortgage into a 15-year mortgage — or less!

After paying off this first house, you could save the monthly payment for a few years, sell your paid-off home, and then upgrade to a nicer home if desired. In fact, by following this plan, the average American family can own their dream house outright in only ten years. By following the traditional plan (buy all the house you can qualify for and make minimum payments), on the other hand, you'll finally pay off the house in thirty years and may still not be in your dream house!

The bottom line is that when it takes $300,000 to purchase a $100,000 house because of debt, debt is your enemy; it's not your friend!

By the way, debt almost always hurts us much more than it seems to on the surface. If you finance a $100,000 mortgage at 8%, it might seem that the house should end up costing $108,000. But it doesn't—as the 8% only applies to people who pay off that house in one year. That's why lending institutions refer to this 8% as the *Annual* Percentage Rate (APR). If you pay for your house over 30 years, you actually pay approximately 200% interest.

Interest is like an iceberg. You can see the tip above the water, but the vast majority of the iceberg remains underwater and unseen.

Automobile Loans

By the way, these examples get progressively worse. What I'm about to describe to you is worse even than wasting $200,000 in interest payments on a house!

If you always have car payments, you'll spend at least $1000 per year in interest. This holds true whether you lease or buy.

At one time, this fact didn't disturb me—because new cars look good, feel good, and smell good. Even I look good in a new car! Therefore I was willing to pay more for these privileges. But one day I decided to put some math to the true cost of always having car payments.

If folks waste $1000 per year in auto interest over their entire 40-year working career, they've just wasted $40,000—right? Wrong.

To understand the true cost, people need to determine what this $1000 per year would have grown to had they invested it over the forty-year period instead of wasting it. If you invested $1000 per year for forty years and were able to average 12% interest, you would end up with approximately $1,000,000 at the end of 40 years. Yes, that says one million dollars!

The only thing that the average American family has to do to become a millionaire family is to change the way they buy cars. You don't have to *earn* a lot of money to become a millionaire—you just have to figure out a way to take the same money that you presently waste on auto interest and redirect it into wise investments. By doing this, you prevent interest from working *against* you and recruit it to work *for* you. This simple adjustment can solve the retirement problem for many.

> Want to be a millionaire family? Just change the way you buy cars...

I'm not saying we should all be millionaires. My point is simply that your financial goals for the future are being hindered, rather then helped, by debt.

Debt is indeed your enemy; it's not your friend!

Credit Cards

Have I mentioned that these examples get progressively worse? What I'm about to share with you is worse even than the two illustrations above!

I love golf, and I've always wanted an Odyssey putter. I think it's the finest putter money can buy. You can get one for around $100. I used to believe that I could purchase a putter on an 18% credit card, resulting in an actual purchase price of $118.

This isn't true for most of us because the majority of people in the United States pay only the minimum monthly payment on their credit cards each month. This in effect disqualifies you from the published interest rate. Let me illustrate.

Ruthie and I had a credit card that was charged to the limit of $5,000. We determined to pay it off long before the October 22 emotional breakdown date I described earlier. So we cut up the card and quit using it. We sent the minimum payment of $100 per month for the next two years. That added up to $2,400. At the end of these two years, we still owed $5,000. This didn't seem possible, so I began to investigate.

On the credit card statement I discovered a box with the heading, "Finance Charge." Written in that box was the sum of $96. I called my creditor and discovered that each time I sent in $100, they were placing $96 (the finance charge) in their back pocket, only giving me credit for sending in $4. In effect, I was paying 96% interest each month.

So credit card math looks like this:

$$\begin{array}{r} \$5000.00 \\ (\textit{minimum}) \quad \underline{-\$100.00} \\ \$4996.00 \end{array}$$

This is not a misprint. Remember, the credit card company only gave me credit for sending in $4.

Incidentally, if I had doubled my minimum payment, I would have still, in effect, been paying 48% each month.

Unfortunately, this story gets worse. I was in the unhealthy habit of sending my monthly payments late. This resulted in an additional $29 late fee being added to my balance. Now the equation looks like:

$$\begin{array}{r} \$5000.00 \\ (\textit{minimum}) \quad \underline{-\$100.00} \\ \$4996.00 \\ (\textit{late fee}) \quad \underline{+\$29.00} \\ \$5025.00 \end{array}$$

Now, thanks to the late fee, I had exceeded my maximum allowable limit, resulting in yet another fee of $29. The equation now reads:

	$5000.00
(*minimum*)	–$100.00
	$4996.00
(*late fee*)	+$29.00
	$5025.00
(*over-limit fee*)	+$29.00
	$5054.00

I started the month owing $5000. I made no new charges and I sent in $100 (late). Now I owe $5054. This is, in effect, over 100% interest each month.

This made me furious. I told the creditor I was mad. "How old are you?" he asked. I replied, "What does that have to do with my anger at being charged more than 96% interest each month?" He insisted that I answer his question. "I'm 32 years old," I said. Then he said something I'll never forget: "You're far too young to have figured out that we're charging you over 96% interest per month."

I cannot be any clearer with you than this creditor was with me. It's a *losing* proposition to pay anything less than the entire balance when using credit cards. All you have to do to pay over 100% interest on your credit cards is consistently pay only the minimum monthly payment and have an occasional late fee.

I'm *not* against the responsible use of credit cards. Though we went without credit cards for about a year, we now have one, which we use sparingly and responsibly. However, experts tell

 Even if you pay off credit card balances each month, you'll probably spend more than if you just used cash.

us that, even if you pay off the balance each month, you likely spend as much as 30% more when using credit cards than you would have had you stuck with cash and checks. This is probably due to the convenience of credit purchasing. It is simply too easy to purchase with plastic.

Therefore, I recommend you consider going without plastic until *all* your debt is paid off. This will give you time to get used to life without the convenience of plastic, thereby breaking any addiction to credit that you may have. It will also enable you to spend less—freeing up more money for debt elimination.

Health Concerns

I recently read in a newspaper that medical doctors have discovered that living in a long-term environment of oppressive debt harms one's health. Such debt causes enough negative stress to hurt your immune system, result-

> Debt doesn't just hurt your financial health; it can hurt a lot more…

ing in increased illness. Dr. Richard Swenson discusses this in his wonderful book, *Margin*, published by NavPress. I highly recommend it.

The Great Commission Becomes The Great Omission

What is the greatest proof of all? How do we know that debt really is our enemy? Why isn't it our friend?

Though the biblical command to spread the gospel is clear, a Christian overloaded with debt is effectively *unable* to finance the Great Commission of our Lord, Jesus Christ.

In the Bible, we're commanded to share the good news of our Lord in three different ways: to live it, to tell it, and to fund it. First, we are to live a lifestyle that will draw people toward Jesus Christ. When a non-Christian sees a Christian, she or he should see a clear *difference* in lifestyle. The lifestyle of the Christian should be filled with love, joy, peace, patience, kindness, good-

> **The Fruit of the Spirit**
>
> "But the fruit of the Spirit is love, joy, peace, patience, kindness, goodness, faithfulness, gentleness, and self-control. Against such things there is no law."
>
> *Galatians 5:22–23*

ness, faithfulness, gentleness, and self-control. This kind of lifestyle is so foreign to the world we live in and clearly points unbelievers to the fact that we're different. This kind of lifestyle may even attract questions from unbelievers, which can be used as a springboard to a verbal testimony.

Second, we are to tell others about Jesus Christ. We should share a verbal testimony of our commitment to Christ with others. If Jesus has ever done something good for you, tell somebody!

Third, we are to finance the Great Commission of our Lord. We are to give money so the message of Jesus can be shared everywhere, both close to home and throughout the world.

Don't make the mistake of choosing only one of the above methods of spreading the gospel. The Bible commands all Christians to use *all three* methods.

Let's discuss the third method. I attended a Promise-Keepers rally at Texas Stadium in Irving a few years ago. One of the inspirational speakers was Ron Blue. Ron is a gifted Christian financial counselor. Ron shared that the average American household had an average of $12,500 of credit card debt. Then he multiplied that number by 70,000 — the number of men attending the rally — to reveal that there was likely over three-quarters of a billion dollars in credit card debt in that stadium at that moment.

These facts astounded me, but the implications of these facts broke my heart. While we Christian families had cumulatively charged up our credit cards to the tune of $875,000,000, and while most of us were paying more than 96% interest on them without even knowing it, the rest of the world was dying and going to hell for all eternity.

Debt can strangle our Christian witness... if we let it.

This should break our hearts and get our attention! If for no other reason, this should prove that debt is our enemy; it is not our friend. These dollars that are being wasted on interest could be going to fund the gospel of Jesus Christ.

This is worse than losing $200,000 in mortgage interest. It's worse than failing to become a millionaire because of the unfortunate choice always to have car payments. This is worse than paying 96% interest on our credit cards. This is worse than the illnesses that come about as a result of stress. This is as bad as it gets. We're talking about the souls of girls, boys, men, and women that are lost for all eternity — and that is an absolute tragedy.

If we could redirect the same money from paying interest on debt to funding the Great Commission of our Lord, we could see many more people won to the Kingdom of God. Now that's *exciting*!

May these examples serve as a permanent reminder that debt is our enemy; it's not our friend!

chapter **2**

Declare War on Your Enemy

Webster's Dictionary defines war as:
1) *a state or period of usually open and declared* fighting;
2) *the art or* science *of warfare;*
3) *a state of* hostility, *conflict, or antagonism;*
4) *a struggle between* opposing forces *for a particular end.*

"...fighting..."

Going to war against debt is not a picnic. It's not a party, a church fellowship, or any other enjoyable activity. It's a fight!

I learned the most about fighting when I was in junior high school. During that period of my life, I got in some fights. I learned some valuable lessons as a result. For example, I learned that even if you win the fight, you often get hurt. You may walk away bleeding, bruised, in pain, and in trouble with the school principal.

If you choose to go to war against debt—even if you win—you'll experience pain. The biblical strategies set forth in this book require sacrifice and commitment. If you were looking for a book about conquering debt the easy way, you picked up the wrong book.

By the way, if you ever see a book titled *Conquering Debt the Easy Way*, don't buy it! It'll be a waste of your money. There is no *easy* way to conquer debt. Every effective debt-elimination strategy is difficult—but that's all right. Once you understand and accept this difficult truth, you'll be able to transcend it.

And believe me, the pain required to eliminate debt is not nearly as devastating as the pain of staying in debt. Of course, while this statement is true, the early months of transitioning from being a debt accumulator to a debt eliminator are quite difficult. But once you've made this transition, you'll be well on your way!

"...science..."

Soon, I'll share with you a scientifically and mathematically sound approach to rapid debt elimination. For the record, I won't be teaching you the two most commonly taught debt-elimination strategies in America. The unconventional strategy I'll share with you is not what is commonly taught by our worldly system. It is, in fact, the *opposite* of what the world teaches.

This strategy will not encourage you to pay off those high interest credit cards first, nor will I encourage you to pay off the smallest balances first. For twelve years, Ruthie and I followed such advice of the world regarding debt elimination. The result was that our total indebtedness did not shrink—it grew!

Then, we committed ourselves to biblical strategies and eliminated all our debt—including our house and car debt—in less than five years! It's *God* who knows how to eliminate debt rapidly, not the world!

"...hostility..."

In my attempts to understand better what war is like, I've asked some who had actually served in wars, such as the Vietnam War, to describe the nature of war. Their descriptions have been enlightening.

I was astounded by these veterans' word choices. Listen to some of the verbs they used: destroy, kill, demolish, cream, drive out, attack, win or die. Now listen to these adjectives: intense, vicious, aggressive, bloody, and brutal. Warriors understand the life-or-death nature of battle: show no mercy; leave no survivors who can turn around and attack you; don't return home until the job gets done.

Approach debt elimination as a soldier approaches battle.

Guess what? I've just told you how to get out of debt! It requires absolute commitment. It requires an attitude of battletude! It requires focus, intensity, and near hostility regarding your enemy—debt.

Even a poor debt-elimination strategy will work—if you're committed. And, even the best debt-elimination strategy will fail if you're not committed. The bottom-line key to success is *your commitment*.

On October 22 a few years ago, I explained to my wife how frustrated I was with life. I was miserable. I was no longer able to take the debt pressure and was willing to do anything God asked me to do in order to defeat it. I came to the conclusion that I was not experiencing the abundant life promised by Jesus.

I no longer cared about the personal cost or personal sacrifices it might take in order to become debt-free. I was willing to do *anything* God asked me to do, even if it cost me my life. I believe strongly that this is the same kind of commitment Joshua made to God. He was willing to go into hostile enemy territory and battle a group of giants who significantly outnumbered his army. He was not concerned about the personal cost, though this commitment could have literally cost him his life. He was simply focused on obedience to God's commands.

My wife responded with similar feelings and a mutual commitment to do *anything* God asked us to do—regardless of the cost. It was on that day that Ruthie and I became serious about debt elimination; all our previous attempts to eliminate debt had merely been game playing.

"...opposing forces..."

There are at least four forces that will fight back at you once you declare war upon debt. They include debt itself, the devil, society, and family and friends.

Debt itself will fight back. Debt loves to rule in your life. Once debt notices your commitment to eliminate it, it will fight you. You'll actually feel a deeper desire and need to use debt than ever before. Debt has most of us trained to think that we *need* it. Be prepared for debt to go to new and extreme measures to remind you of your inability to survive without it. Debt will try to convince you that it is your friend and not your enemy. It is critical that you resist debt as it attempts to dissuade you.

The devil will fight you, too. Do you think the devil wants you to be so financially free that you're able to be a contagious, generous, hilarious, outrageous, and spontaneous contributor to the kingdom of God and to others in need? Of course not!

Many who apply the principles in this book will soon easily be able to give away $10,000 cash to God's kingdom or a deserving charity. How do I know? Because many who read this already have $2000 per *month* of debt (or more). Add up your house payment, your car payments, your credit card payments, your medical debts, your department store charge card payments, your debt-consolidation note, your second mortgage, your personal loans, and your student education loans. It adds up, doesn't it?

As soon as you get everything paid for—it takes the average American family 5 years using these exciting strategies—you may have $2000 per month left over! Just imagine. Not a one-time refund from the IRS or a one-time gift from a relative. We're talking about extra money every month!

If you choose to, you could save all that extra money for five months and then give it away! It's entirely doable for the average middle class working family to be

> Conquering debt can give you the money you need for a life of hilarious generosity.

hilariously generous in giving. And after this gift, you could use the $2000 per month for such expenses as college funds for children (or grandchildren—take note, Mom and Dad!), wedding funds for your children (I have three daughters), retirement funds, dream house funds, funds to start a business, travel funds, or whatever God leads you to!

I repeat my question: do you think the devil wants you to be able to be a contagious, generous, hilarious, outrageous, and spontaneous contributor? No! The devil wants you in a financial straitjacket. I believe that the devil uses debt more than any other means in our country today to render Christians powerless to face some of the more important issues of life—such as giving and saving for future needs—by locking them in a financial prison.

In addition to debt and the devil, society fights back against debt elimination! There's one company—I won't reveal its name—but this company claims that it pays to *discover*. It does *not* pay to "discover." The opposite is actually the truth. It costs! It may cost you 96% interest per month; it may cost you the ability to sleep well; it may cost you peace in your heart; it may cost you your family. Do you know what the number one destroyer of marriages is? Financial problems, usually brought about by excessive debt. We live in a society that regularly communicates untrue messages to us. You are, and will continue to be, bombarded by them in newspapers, magazines, billboards, and television.

Family and friends will also fight you. I don't think they always do it intentionally, but they do fight back.

Here's one way they do it: they go buy a new car and then they come by your house.

One day we heard a knock at our front door. Upon opening the door, I recognized the man as a personal friend, so I invited him in. He said, "No, I don't want to come in, but I would like you to come out." He then proceeded to show me his brand-new $38,000 Ford Expedition.

During this experience, I did my best to follow the biblical command to "rejoice with those who rejoice." But deep down inside, I was really hoping that a severe hailstorm would come by and nail his vehicle before he returned home.

I'm really not a bad person—just an envious one. Envy prevented me from rejoicing with him and actually encouraged me to wish harm upon his new vehicle. Envy further tempted me to go purchase my dream vehicle—a $44,000 Suburban with leather interior. I wanted to take it by his house the next day so I could show him my new bigger, badder, better vehicle. I could have financially "afforded" to do just that. But to do so would have required new debt.

> "Rejoice with those who rejoice; mourn with those who mourn. Live in harmony with one another. Do not be proud, but be willing to associate with people of low position. Do not be conceited. Do not repay anyone evil for evil. Be careful to do what is right in the eyes of everybody. If it is possible, as far as it depends on you, live at peace with everyone."
>
> *Romans 12:15–18*

> "A heart at peace gives life to the body, but envy rots the bones!"
>
> *Proverbs 14:30*

Therefore, I didn't go purchase my dream vehicle. I continued to drive my 15-year-old car that had 150,000 miles on it. I did it voluntarily so I could use every spare penny to focus on debt elimination!

If you commit to the strategies in this book, you will likely be able to afford your dream vehicle within six months, with money you free up from aggressive debt elimination. However, if you are ever to become completely debt free, you'll need to make the same choice I made. *Voluntarily* choose to drive much less vehicle than you can technically afford so you can use every possible penny to eliminate debt.

While I trust the dictionary's definition of war, I trust the Word of God even more! Let's look at God's definition of the kind of war it takes to leave the land of bondage and enter the land of blessing.

Joshua 10:9–40

To make a point, I am only quoting selected words and phrases from this text.

9   *Joshua came upon them suddenly by marching all night from Gilgal.*

10 *He slew them, …great slaughter, …pursued them, …struck them…*

11 *the LORD threw large stones from heaven on them and they died…*

16 *five kings … hid themselves…*

19 *pursue your enemies and attack them in the rear. Do not allow them to enter their cities…*

20 *…finished slaying them with a very great slaughter, until they were all destroyed…*

24 *"Come near, put your feet on the necks of these kings."*

26 *Joshua struck them and put them to death, and hanged them on five trees and they hung on the trees until evening.*

27 *…took them down and threw them into the cave…*

28 *captured Makkedah…struck it…its king…edge of the sword; utterly destroyed it and every person who was in it. He left no survivor. Thus he did to the king of Makkedah just as he had done to the king of Jericho.*

29 *…passed on from Makkedah to Libnah, and fought against Libnah.*

30 *And the LORD gave it…he struck it and every person who was in it with the edge of the sword. He left no survivor in it. Thus he did to its king just as he had done to the king of Jericho.*

31 *He passed on from Mastercard to Visa and they camped by it and fought against it [whoops—loose paraphrase].*

32 *...captured it...struck it and every person who was in it with the edge of the sword...*

33 *Then Horam king of Gezer came up to help Lachish, and Joshua defeated him and his people until he had left him no survivor.*

34 *...from Lachish to Eglon, and they camped by it and fought against it.*

35 *...captured...struck it with the edge of the sword; and he utterly destroyed that day every person who was in it...*

36 *...from Eglon to Hebron...fought...*

37 *...captured...struck...edge of the sword...no survivor...utterly destroyed...*

38 *...to Debir...fought...*

39 *...captured...struck...edge of the sword...utterly destroyed...no survivor...*

40 *Thus Joshua struck all the land, the hill country, the Negev and the lowland and the slopes and all their kings. He left no survivor, but he utterly destroyed all who breathed, just as the LORD, the God of Israel, had commanded.*

Wow! God makes warfare plain, doesn't he? This is the kind of war you can expect once you declare war against debt.

Biblical Keys to Success

First, Joshua succeeded because he recognized that God had commanded him to fight this war. Likewise, we need to recognize that God has commanded us to fight the war against debt. Second, Joshua pursued his enemies. Though they ran and hid, he pursued. Your debt will run and hide from you, but it is your job to pursue it. Do not give up. Do not give out. *Persevere!*

This book is not about my opinion on debt. It's about God's commands concerning debt. A simple biblical under-standing of God's teaching about debt shows the following:

> The Bible does not prohibit debt. This is probably because there are a few occasions when debt actu-ally makes sense—for example, the purchase of your

first house. But these exceptions are so few, and God always speaks of debt in negative terms. For example, in Proverbs 22:7, the Bible says "the borrower is a slave to the lender." In other words, if you want to be a slave, borrow money. Have you thought about that? It's possible to live in a free country and still be a slave.

❯ If you have debt, pay it back! Psalm 37:21 says "it is the wicked who borrow and do not repay." We not only have a legal obligation to repay our debts; we have a moral and ethical obligation to pay back our lenders. This means that if there's any way humanly possible, do what it takes to pay off your debts.

❯ Pay off your debts as fast as possible! In America, you can get a 30-year mortgage on your house. It can be even worse in Japan, where you can get a *90-year* mortgage on a house. They call these third-generational loans. But in the Bible, the longest loan term you can find is seven years! What does this fact mean for us today? I think it means that God never intended us to live in an environment of long-term, oppressive debt. So we should feel a sense of urgency and pay off debts as fast as possible.

> In the Bible, the longest term for a loan is seven years...

Again, this is God's command for his children, not my opinion about debt. We need to feel a real sense of responsibility to God and his Word regardless of what the world teaches about debt!

How to Declare War Against Debt

I want to ask you to consider the power of making a vow to God. The Bible has much to say about making vows. Repeatedly in the Bible, the term is used to refer to a promise or pledge, and the Bible emphasizes that such vows are binding. Few scriptural principles are clearer than that of keeping vows—keeping our word to God and others—and the clear message of Scripture is that when we give our word to do something, we're obligated to *do* it.

Yet not everyone is convinced that making vows is proper. In his booklet *Five Vows for Spiritual Power*, A. W. Tozer writes,

> Some people object to vows, but in the Bible you will find many great men of God directed by covenants, promises, vows, and pledges. A carnal man refuses the discipline of such commitments. He says, "I want to be free. [Vows are] legalism." There are many religious tramps in the world who will not be bound by anything.

Vows are one of the ways that God's people show their faith, and the Bible is full of advice about making them. Consider the following examples:

> *Make vows to the LORD your God and fulfill them.* Psalm 76:11

> *Offer to God a sacrifice of thanksgiving and pay your vows to the Most High; and call upon Me in the day of trouble; I shall rescue you, and you will honor Me.* Psalm 50:14–15

> *When you make a vow to the LORD your God, you shall not delay to pay it, for it would be sin in you, and the LORD your God will surely require it of you.* Deuteronomy 23:21

> *You shall be careful to perform what goes out from your lips, just as you have voluntarily vowed to the LORD your God what you have promised.* Deuteronomy 23:23

While we certainly shouldn't enter into vows lightly, we should also not overlook their usefulness in helping us to conquer debt!

 For other passages about vows, see Numbers 30:2, Psalm 22:25, and Ecclesiastes 5: 4–5. Proverbs 20:25 warns not to enter into vows impulsively, or you'll regret it later…

The idea behind making a vow to God is to lock yourself voluntarily into certain actions before the moment of temptation strikes.

You must make committed decisions *before* you stumble into a moment of weakness.

A good illustration of preparing in advance for temptation is found in the "True Love Waits" campaign. This campaign has swept our nation during the last 20 years. It's designed for teenagers and college students for the purpose of encouraging them to practice sexual abstinence until their wedding night.

Churches and other groups teach the biblical principles, the practical reasons, and the benefits of sexual abstinence. Then at the end of the campaign, participants are asked to sign a vow to God, expressing their commitment to follow his plan. Participants often express their commitments in a public way such as an official committal ceremony, placing their cards on the altars of their churches during a public invitation, or placing their commitment cards on bulletin boards for others to see. Teenagers and college students all over our country are succeeding in saving themselves sexually for their spouses as a result.

Why has this campaign been so successful? Because if you know where you stand before temptation strikes, if you're committed to your stance, if you've signed a vow

Don't wait until you're tempted to make a commitment...

to God expressing your commitment, and you've gone public with your commitment, you can emerge victorious!

Ruthie and I decided to use the power of signing a vow to God as a practical way to express our official declaration of war against debt. This strategy alone led us to a clear and focused commitment! Don't forget—commitment is the key to success. The vow we signed asks you to commit to the following:

See the "Vow to Declare War on Debt" on page 133. Feel free to photocopy this to use in your own battle...

> *No longer accept just getting by from paycheck to paycheck.*

After paying all our debts each month Ruthie and I used

to place them in their envelopes on a small table near the front door of our home. We wouldn't mail them. The reason was that our bank account had a zero balance. We had to wait until the next payday in order to mail the month's bills. When payday arrived, we were able to mail our payments. However, this left us with a zero balance once again. We had money in our account for only 5 minutes. Signing this vow is a commitment to escape this kind of lifestyle as rapidly as possible.

> *Make rapid debt elimination your primary financial objective.* If you sign this vow and you get an IRS refund, where does it go? Debt elimination! The same holds true with salary raises, bonuses, garage sales, surprise money, etc. Don't sign this if you're not willing to follow through in every way.

> *Commit yourselves without reservation to conquering debt God's way.* Don't let any circumstances interfere with your complete follow-through. You won't be as excited about debt elimination in 6 months as you are today. Never mind; that doesn't matter. Once you've signed this vow, you've *obligated* yourselves to follow through — even when you don't feel like it.

> *Attack debt with a passion.* We believed that God might choose to cancel our debts miraculously. However, we also realized that it took time to get into debt — and that it would most likely take time to get out as well. Whether by miracle or by dogged determination, we committed to be debt-free. "Dogged determination" is best seen in the life of a certain type of dog. A pit bull knows that its goal when fighting is to grab its victim by the throat. It also knows that once it has its victim by the throat, it is never to let go unless one of two things occur: either the victim or the pit bull dies. The pit bull knows that

death must occur before it lets go. When you sign this vow, you are saying that you are going to grab debt by the throat, and that you will never let go until your debt dies or until you die trying. Do not sign this oath if you don't mean it!

You'll notice that the "Vow to Declare War on Debt" has a place for two signatures for those who are married. It's *imperative* that a husband and wife make this commitment together. If only one spouse is committed to this process, it's virtually impossible to succeed. Unless both of you are willing to sign, neither of you should. But if both of you sign this commitment, you're agreeing to work together. You're agreeing to make sacrifices. You are acknowledging the fact that debt is your

> It's important for spouses to work together in conquering debt — otherwise, there's no way to succeed.

enemy—*not* each other. And you are committing to work together as a team to eliminate debt the destroyer.

Why is a Signature Important?

Your signature is more valuable than you may know. There was a day in our society when you could borrow money for a mortgage on a handshake. That's no longer true. Now everybody wants your signature. When paying by check, a signature is required. When applying for a credit card, a signature is required. When you sign something, you're expressing commitment on the highest level recognized by our culture. Your signature can even be used against you in a court of law. When you sign something, you're expected to make good on it.

Most people hesitate before signing anything requiring a commitment, which is a good thing. You should never sign something nonchalantly. Always think twice and pray before signing anything. And when you do sign something, follow through! It's your responsibility!

When God called me to sign the vow we've included on page 135, I balked. I didn't want to sign anything related to my relationship with God. Essentially, God was saying, "Bruce, you've been expressing your commitment to humankind through your signature for years. You've signed many loan papers, credit card applications, and mortgage agreements. I want *at least* the same commitment you've been pledging to mankind—sign a vow to Me and follow through on it."

God went on to convince me that I had gotten into my debt mess by signing vows—and meaning them. Similarly, the way out of my debt mess was to sign vows and mean them. After signing our vow, we made two copies. We placed one on our bathroom mirror as a daily reminder of our commitment. We gave the second copy to our pastor as a public expression of our commitment.

Remember, the dictionary says that war is "open and declared." You cannot successfully fight a war in private. It is critical that you go public. In some church traditions, it may be more appropriate for you to give a copy of the vow to an elder than to some other mentor. Whatever the case, God has chosen human representatives for your church. Going public with this person is another form of commitment. Additionally, he or she will most likely pray regularly for you as you follow through on your commitment to God.

 Tell a trusted church leader about your war on debt.

If you're unwilling to follow this step, I seriously doubt your level of commitment to debt elimination. In fact, if you're unwilling to "go public," you might as well stop reading this book now. Why? Because what I've just asked you to do is the easiest strategy in this book. It just gets more difficult as we proceed. However, remaining in debt is worse than even the hardest thing I'll ask you to do. And the benefits of commitment are absolutely worth it.

Remember the reality of $2000 extra per month. What would you do with all that money? Any time you're considering a commitment, it is critical to focus on the personal benefits resulting from the commitment. Though the difficult aspects need to be understood and considered before "signing on" to anything, once you're on board, think regularly about the benefits!

The model for this behavior is Jesus Christ himself. In Hebrews 12:2 we read, "it was for the joy set before him that Jesus endured the cross." Though the cross was a painful and excruciating experience, the Bible says that Jesus was able to endure because of the "joy set before him." Jesus could see beyond the pain to the great joy that would be his by making a way for an eternal relationship with you. Jesus enjoys a very personal relationship with those who believe in him and who receive him as their Lord and Savior, and his joy in this relationship comes because of his sacrifice on the cross!

Don't think of the sacrifices involved in debt elimination. Think of the many benefits you'll enjoy once the war is won!

chapter **3**

Demonstrate Fearless Faith

What is it that you need the most in order to get out of debt? The answer is money! Brace yourself! I'm about to ask you to give away the very thing you need the most. Though this makes no sense to the human, finite mind, it's actually a brilliant battle strategy.

Think through the story of Joshua winning the battle of Jericho (Joshua 6). God asked Joshua to drop the very thing he needed the most—his weapons. God then instructed Joshua and his army to pick up trumpets and march around the walls while playing some pretty music. This strategy makes no sense whatsoever to the human mind. However, it was actually a test. God was testing Joshua to see if Joshua really trusted him or if Joshua simply *claimed* to trust him.

Of course, Joshua really did trust and obey God in spite of his inability to understand the strategy. Now, *that's* fearless faith! When you obey God's instruction—even when it makes no sense to you—you're demonstrating fearless faith, too. The rewards of Joshua's true faith resulted in a miraculous victory at Jericho. God himself supernaturally intervened in this battle, knocked the walls of Jericho down, and secured victory for God's people. The results of true faith on your part will bear great results. When you pass the fearless faith test, God himself gets involved in your finances, knocks down the walls of your debt, and secures financial victory for you.

The Word "Tithe"

To start out, it's probably important to establish something. When I use the word "tithe," I'm simply referring to giving away 10% of your income to God through your local church.

To Tithe First or to Eliminate Debt First?

When I first began to grapple with these issues, I remember saying to God, "God, if you'll help me get out of debt, I'll start tithing." God's response to me was clear: "If you'll start tithing, I'll help you out of debt."

> To get out of debt, you must start by giving your money away — to God.

Take a Deep Breath and Relax!

Before I go any further, I think I need to remind you that you *don't* have to tithe and give offerings. This is not something God makes you do. It's not likely that your minister makes you tithe. I trust that the fact that you have an option here helps you to relax. Please relax! What I'll show you in this chapter shouldn't make you uptight. The fact is—you don't have to do this if you don't want to.

However, you may want to tithe and give offerings. Let me tell you why. Did you know that the fastest way to get out of debt is to tithe right off the top of your income? Did you know that the fastest way to reach your retirement goals is to tithe right off the top? Did you know that 90% of your income with the blessing of God will go further than 100% of your income without God's blessing? The fact is that you're better off financially if you tithe than if you don't.

You may be thinking, "Oh no, not another health, wealth, and prosperity preacher." I'm not a health, wealth, and prosperity preacher. But facts are facts—when you enlist God's supernatural involvement in your finances, you'll be better off financially. I'll show you what I mean....

Important Bible Words

Believe

Did you know that the word "believe" appears in the Bible 272 times? This is a very important word. In fact, it's so important that if you don't figure this one out, you go to hell when you die!

Pray

"Pray" appears in the Bible 371 times, and thus is also a very important word. The quality of your relationship with God will be determined to a large degree by the quality of your prayer life—both speaking to God and listening to God.

Love

The word "love" is found in the Bible 714 times. First Corinthians 13:13 says "...faith, hope, and love remain—but the greatest of these is love."

Give

This word is found in Scripture 2,162 times. Wow!

God's Repetition

I have a question for you. How many times does God have to say something to make it true? Once, of course. In that case, why does he choose to repeat himself?

God repeats himself for the sake of emphasis! There are some things that are so important to God that he repeats himself often so we won't miss a blessing. Yet even with God's repetition, Americans still don't get the message. The average American gives away only 2% of his or her income to churches or charity.

Why Does God Want Me To Give?

I remember asking, "God, do you need my money?" God replied, "No, I don't need your money. I'm not a financially needy God. In fact, I'm a financially wealthy God." I said, "God, I *do* need my money. Since I need it and you don't, I think I'll just keep it." God answered, "You're missing the point."

I remember saying, "God, I bet you want me to give so the staff at my church can get paid." God said, "No, that's not the reason I want you to give. Though I will use your gifts to pay the staff, that's not the primary reason I want you to give."

I said, "It must be so we can maintain our buildings, keep the utilities paid, and build more buildings as necessary." God said, "No — though I will use your gifts for such things, that's not the primary reason I want you to give."

I said, "It must be so we can send out missionaries to win others to Christ." God said, "Though I will use your gifts for evangelism and missions, that isn't the primary reason I want you to give either."

"Then why do you want me to give?" I'll never forget what God said. He replied, "Bruce, I want you to give because giving blesses you. It benefits you, changes you, improves you, and helps you. It flips a switch on the inside of you without which you probably

Tithing brings many exciting benefits from God.

wouldn't get out of debt." This was an entirely new concept to me. I was beginning to realize that God has many special blessings in store for givers. To refuse to tithe was to refuse these blessings.

Blessings That Come to Tithers and Offering Givers

In a recent class, Rick Warren of the Saddleback Community Church in Lake Forest, California pointed out several blessings that come to those who tithe:

Giving Makes Us More Like God

John 3:16 says, "For God so loved the world that He gave his only begotten son...." God is a giver! From the first page of the Bible to the last, one thing you see is a generous, giving God. One of God's purposes for his children is for us to become more like him (see Romans 8:29). We must become givers to become more like God—and becoming more like God is a wonderful benefit for anyone!

Giving Draws Us Closer to God

One of the greatest benefits of conquering debt God's way is drawing closer to God. Many families have paid off every debt to their names, including house and cars. Upon their arrival in "Debt-Free Land," many have told me that being debt-free pales in comparison to the closer walk with God they now enjoy. It's not that "Debt-Free Land" is less than they anticipated. It's that their newfound, fresh-and-alive relationship with God is *more* than they ever imagined.

Think back to that time when you were closer to God than ever before. Remember how you anticipated time with him in the Word and in prayer? Remember when you were excited about sharing your faith? Those were sweet days.

The Bible teaches that the first thing we should do when we want to turn back to God as the priority relationship of our lives is to tithe and give offerings.

Read Malachi 3:6–12. Notice that God is calling a people who have strayed from him to come back to him. These people ask him how to return. He responds, "in tithes and offerings." God promises a renewed fellowship and a freshness of relationship to those who obey—the most wonderful benefits of giving.

In my Day Planner, I carry a very special one-dollar bill. On a recent Father's Day, it was given to me by my daughter Carlee. Though I don't need this dollar, it's the most valuable dollar I've ever possessed. I've cried joyful tears many times when reflecting on this experience. And I carry this dollar with me everywhere I go. When Carlee gave it to me, it was *all she had*. She didn't have to give it to me in order to qualify to be my daughter. She chose to give it to me because she loved me. This expression of love created a closeness in our relationship that we couldn't experience any other way. Giving always brings a closeness and a special quality to a relationship. This is also true in our relationship with God. Incidentally, Carlee's act created a desire in me to be even more generous with her than ever!

Giving Is the Antidote to Materialism

1 Timothy 6:17–19 says the following (pay special attention to the emphasized words):

> *Command those who are* rich *in this present world not to be arrogant nor to put their hope in wealth, which is so uncertain, but to put their hope in God who richly provides us with everything for our* enjoyment. *Command them to… be generous and willing to share. In this way they…may take hold of the life that is* truly life.

> ❯ *Rich*: most of us would not define ourselves as rich. However, consider the following information. There are now over 6 billion people on earth. Over half of these live off of less than $2 per day. If you make more than $2 per day, you're already in the top 50% of the world's most wealthy people. If you happen to have one automobile, you've now entered into the top 10%

of the world's most wealthy people. If you have two automobiles, you're now in the top 5% of the world's most wealthy people.

Even those who live at poverty level in America today are wealthy by the world's standards. Most Americans who live below the poverty line still have a place to live, a car to drive, and a television to watch (maybe one connected to cable)! My wife and I have lived below the poverty line in this country and even then we were in the top 5% of the world's most wealthy people.

The truth is, most of the world would love to have your problems. They would love to trade places with you. They would even love to have your debt. They have different problems than we do in this country. They struggle with issues such as finding food for a starving child or finding medical care for a critically ill child. In this country, you have access to food and medical care even if you have no money. How can this be? Because we're rich. That's how. God convinced me that if the word "rich" ever applied to a people, it applies to Americans today!

> *Enjoy*: I have good news for you. The Bible teaches that you have God's permission to enjoy the riches he has given you. You don't have to feel guilty because you have enough money to live in a nice house or to eat out. God has given you riches for your enjoyment.

> *True life*: Everyone I know, whether a believer in Jesus Christ or not, is looking for a meaningful life, an abundant life, a fulfilling life, a true life. God teaches that this most elusive discovery is reserved only for those who are "generous and willing to share."

You do not have to agree with, like, or even believe in this fact, yet it remains true. You can be a born-again believer in Jesus Christ, and on your way to heaven when you die, and still miss abundant life here on Earth. True life comes from being a generous giver. Winston Churchill said, "We make a living by what we get, but we make a life by what we give."

You don't have to tithe and give offerings if you don't want to. However, if you want to experience true life, meaningful life, fulfilling life, and abundant life, you do—because true life comes from being a generous giver!

Giving Demonstrates Our Faith

You can say you have faith all day long, but unless you demonstrate it, you don't have it. The Bible teaches that

Do: trust in the Lord with all your heart.
Don't: lean upon your own understanding.

faith is always demonstrated. For example, Proverbs 3:5–9 teaches us there is something we are to do—and something we are to "don't." Then we are given a test. The do is: do trust in the Lord with all your heart. The don't is: don't lean upon your own understanding.

The reason God doesn't want us to lean upon our own understanding is that we're not nearly as smart as we think we are. Consider this: a recent attempt to send a satellite to Mars failed. When asked why this $128,000,000 project failed, a NASA rocket scientist answered, "a mathematical error." This should alert even the most intelligent among us that we're not nearly as smart as we think we are. Some of our most brilliant thinkers still make mathematical errors—even with the help of computer technology.

The Bible is the ultimate knowledge book. However, it warns us not to make even that knowledge the foundation of our lives. We are to make our trust in God the foundation of our lives.

When Joshua was confronted with dropping his weapons at Jericho, it made no sense to his human understanding. However, he chose to obey the Lord anyway. He was not leaning upon his own understanding. He was trusting in the Lord! As a result, God knocked down the walls of Jericho before him and enabled him to achieve a swift victory!

Like Joshua, our trust in God was challenged in our battle. Tithing off the top of our income made no sense to my wife and me, but we decided not to lean on our own understanding. Instead, we trusted in the Lord. As a result, God knocked down the walls of our debt before us and gave us victory, too!

Giving Off of the Top Honors God

If you honor God off the top of your income, you're demonstrating to God (and yourself) that you've built the foundation of your life upon trust in the Lord. If you don't honor God with the top of your income, you're demonstrating to God (and yourself) that you've built the foundation of your life upon your own understanding—your human reasoning.

It's easy to tithe off the bottom of your income, but difficult to tithe off the top of your income. Here's why: if your intent is to tithe off the bottom, you're basically saying "God, I'm going to take care of all my needs first, and if there's 10% left over, I'll give it to you." This takes no faith because if you have 10% left over, you give it. If you don't have 10% left over, you can't give it. No faith is required.

However, it takes faith to tithe off the top of your income, thus communicating to God: "God, I'm going to write my first check after payday to you. As I do this, I'm not sure that I'll be able to afford to take care of my needs. But, by this very action, I'm trusting by faith that you're going to take care of all my needs."

Giving Is an Investment for Eternity

1 Timothy 6:18–19 also says that giving is "the only safe investment for eternity."

Many invest in everything—except what really counts. We want to fully fund our 401(k) and our IRA. We want to invest in stocks, bonds, and real estate. When we do these things, we're investing in everything except what really counts. While there's nothing wrong with these kinds of investments, when we fund them before we invest in the kingdom of God, we have our priorities reversed.

The Bible makes it clear: there's only one investment that is safe and that can make a difference for all eternity. That investment involves giving money away to the kingdom of God.

Giving Blesses Us in Return

Think about the message of these scriptures:

A generous man will himself be blessed. Proverbs 22:9

A generous man will prosper; he who refreshes others will himself be refreshed. Proverbs 11:25

Good will come to him who is generous. Psalm 112:5

Giving is for us, it blesses us, it benefits us, it helps us, it improves us, it changes us, it flips a switch inside of us without which we would probably not get out of debt nor stay out of debt.

But there's another message here as well. Some of you (though not all of you) would be making twice as much in salary today had you been tithing during the past year. God promises to bless us when we obey him. Sometimes his blessings are financial in nature, and sometimes his blessings are even better than financial. On occasion, when he chooses to bless us financially, he overwhelms us with his generosity. I know of an insurance salesman whose salary jumped from $40,000 to $80,000 the first year he started tithing. I know of a commercial real estate agent whose income more than doubled the year after he started

"Tithing off the top" brings great blessings—and can increase your income, too.

tithing. And then there's the building contractor whose salary went from $50,000 to $100,000 the first year after he committed to tithe. The next year his salary doubled again to $200,000! I know of a gentleman employed by a newspaper company whose income quadrupled within 3 months after he committed to tithe.

Do you know what disturbs me about these stories? After I started tithing, my salary didn't double. And I think I know why. I believe that God wants to make sure I don't miscommunicate his truth. God doesn't promise to double our income. He just promises to bless us somehow! Sometimes God's blessings are financial. When they are, we can use the increase to help us wage our war on debt. And when his blessings are not financial, we still enjoy and appreciate them immensely.

It's not our job to tell God what kind of blessings we prefer. It's our job to obey God, and trust that he knows what kinds of blessing would be best for us.

Giving Makes Us Happy!

I did a wedding for a young couple several years ago. Because they were very poor, I didn't expect to receive an honorarium from them. After the wedding, the father of the bride handed me an envelope. When I got to my car, I opened it. Inside was a $100 bill.

As I drove home, I asked myself, "What am I going to do with this money?" Then it dawned on me: I could use it to buy that Odyssey putter I had always wanted. But God had other ideas. He began to impress me that I should turn around and go back to the church and give this $100 to that young, poor couple.

At this point, I began to reason with God. I had a hundred reasons why I should keep this money for myself. God didn't argue with me, but he did repeat himself. I decided to obey. Shortly after this experience, I received a thank you note from the young couple. It said: "Bruce, thank you for your generous gift and all you've done for us. Our honeymoon would have been a flop without your gift. We won't forget you."

Wow! That made me happy! I had turned a "Burger King" night into a "Red Lobster" night for them. And it didn't just make me happy then; it still makes me happy now. In fact, I think I'm even happier about it now than I was then. It seems that God is paying me compound interest on my happiness.

What would have happened if I had disobeyed God? I would have bought that Odyssey putter, and I would still shoot the same sorry golf I always shoot. But I obeyed God, and he made me happy! The fact that happiness comes with generosity shouldn't surprise us. After all, Jesus said, "There is more happiness in giving than in receiving" (Acts 20:35).

Look over the benefits of giving described above. Notice that none of them say anything about paying the preacher, building buildings, or sending missionaries. Though these things are wonderful, the blessings are all for you and your benefit!

As I said, God doesn't need your money. You don't have to tithe and give offerings. But if you want the wonderful blessings described above—you do have to! Tithing and giving offerings "qualifies" you for blessings such as these—and more!

Why Debt-Free Living Comes Faster to Tithers than Non-Tithers

Malachi 3:6–12 teaches us several reasons that tithing actually accelerates your debt elimination success.

Tithing Opens the Windows to God's Blessings

Though this next illustration takes a little imagination, the principles it teaches are true.

The Bible teaches us that there are windows in Heaven. I want you to imagine one of those windows having your name written on it. Imagine that inside the window is the most beautifully decorated Christmas tree you've ever seen. Underneath the tree are more gifts than you could ever imagine. These gifts represent the blessings that God wants to give you. He wants to unlock this window of Heaven, open it, and invite you to enjoy the gift of all these blessings. Some of these may be financial blessings.

However, the Bible teaches that there are two requirements that we must meet before God overwhelms us with his blessings: we must tithe and give offerings.

Tithing Ensures that God Will Bind the Devourer for Us

The Bible teaches that Satan is the Devourer, and he has God's permission to devour our salary unless we tithe and give offerings.

Let me be clear. You have to give *more* than 10% to obtain these blessings. God wants you to give regular offerings as well as your tithe. In Malachi 3, God says we must do *both*. In the Bible, tithing is the beginning point of giving. But God wants us to give above and beyond 10%.

While obeying God by giving the tithe and offerings does bring wonderful blessings, it doesn't mean that all of our problems will go away. It doesn't even mean that all of our financial problems will go away. Even though we tithe and give offerings, we'll still have some financial problems. But this fact doesn't negate the truth that God really protects the salary of those who tithe and give offerings.

Let me illustrate. If you tithe and give offerings, the tires on your automobile will still wear out. However, if you tithe and give offerings, I believe they won't wear out as fast. This illustrates that we can have both God's protection on our salary and still have financial problems. Both facts are true, and one does not negate the other. But one thing is certain — you'll be better off financially in the long run if you tithe and give offerings!

Tithing Helps Us Defeat Our Selfishness

Why are most people in debt in the first place? Because of selfishness. Therefore, if we are to get out of debt, we have to get rid of the thing that brought us there. We must overcome selfishness. How do we overcome selfishness? By giving money away.

As you give, you'll be placing a dagger in the heart of your selfishness. This will help you overcome impulsive, selfish credit purchasing, which will in turn increase your debt-elimination effectiveness.

What are the Specifics of Tithing?

Tithing is:

> Commanded by God (Leviticus 27:30).

> Commended by Jesus (Matthew 23:23). Jesus only commended the Pharisees once in the entire Bible. It was much more common to find him reprimanding

These specifics about tithing are reiterated in the vow on page 135.

them or calling them a "brood of vipers." However, on this one occasion, he commends them as having done one thing right — they had tithed. Please notice that this is from the New Testament; tithing is *not* solely an Old Testament concept.

❯ An opportunity to prove we really love God (John 14:
15). My wife and I still write each other love notes.
Though we've been married for 20 years, it amazes me
how good a love note makes me feel. Let's face it: it feels
great to know you're loved, and it feels even better when
that love has been expressed in writing.

　　When you write your tithe check, it's like writing a
love note to God. As I was writing my last tithe check,
I was expressing the following message to God in my
heart: "Dear God, Have I told you how much I love you
lately? Have I told you how much I cherish you? Have I
told you how much I treasure you? Have I told you that
of all the relationships in the universe, none compares
to the way I feel about you? Love, Bruce."

❯ Ten percent of our gross income (Malachi 3:10). To
give more than 10% is more than tithing. To give less
than 10% is less than tithing. And when we figure
our tithe, we need to figure it on our gross income,
not our net income. When I refer to gross income,
I am referring to one's total income *before* income
taxes are taken out. You might wonder why we use
the gross income figure. The biblical answer is clear.
God wants us to tithe out of the "first fruits," not out
of the leftovers. It would make no sense at all for
us to subtract our rent before figuring the tithe, yet
that's exactly what we do when we tithe off of our
net income. Paying income taxes is nothing more
than paying rent for the privilege of living in America. Some people claim that we live in a free country.
However, the truth is that it costs a lot to live here!
We shouldn't subtract our taxes — our rent — before
we figure the tithe. God said "Bring the *whole* 10%
into the storehouse."

If you own your own business, I encourage you to separate your business bank account from your personal bank account. You would, of course, pay yourself a salary from the business account to the personal account on a regular basis. You would then tithe off of the gross salary amount on the personal side. The business side would look a little different. If the business is operating the way we want it to, it should look like this:

gross receipts
– legitimate expenses
= profit

If the business shows a profit at the end of the year, I believe you should tithe on the profit from the business bank account as well. Of course, you should continue to tithe off of your gross salary each pay period too, and you should do this even if the business takes a loss for the year. By tithing from both your gross personal salary and your business profits, you'll be honoring the Lord in all of the ways that he's prospered you!

> If you own a business, don't just tithe on your salary; tithe on your business profit as well...

> A demonstration that God has first place in our lives (Deuteronomy 14:23).

> To be given to our place of worship with no strings attached (Malachi 3:8–10). Where do we give the tithe? I don't think we have a choice. I'm convinced that it should go to the place where we worship. By the way, this point is costing my ministry a lot of money! I had a friend who once asked me "Is your ministry a 501(c)3 non-profit organization?" When I told him it was, he said, "Then I'm going to send my tithe to your ministry." This put me between a rock and a hard place,

because our ministry needed the financial support and he made in excess of $120,000 per year—meaning this man was offering to send our ministry over $12,000 each year. Yet I believe that the tithe should go to the local church where the tither attends. I shared my convictions with this friend, and he graciously agreed to tithe to his church instead of to my ministry. I realize that there are many rationalizations that lead people to do otherwise. In fact, my friend told me that his church was so well-off financially that it didn't need his money. And my ministry *did* need the money. However, that doesn't change the fact that the Lord has established the local church as the foundational ministry center for the world—and that's where our tithe needs to go.

Please notice that I've also mentioned that there shouldn't be any strings attached. I believe that we should not even designate our tithe within our local church. To do so would violate one of the very lessons God is trying to teach us through tithing.

If I go to a restaurant, pull out a $5 bill, give it to the owner and say, "I want to give this money to your restaurant. Use it however it's needed," what have I just done? I've given money away. If instead I say, "I want to give this money to your restaurant. However, in exchange for this money, I'd like a cheeseburger, an order of fries, and a chocolate malt," what have I just done? This isn't giving; it's shopping. The primary difference between giving and shopping is that when I'm giving, I let go of the money. When I'm shopping, I direct the money.

When we designate the money we "give" to the church, we're not giving at all. We're shopping. We must overcome this desire to shop—to control or to be the boss—and really give this money away. Learning to really let go of money is one of the primary reasons God wants us to tithe in the first place.

After we've tithed 10% of our gross income to our local church with no strings attached, we're ready to enter into the "offering zone" — that is, money beyond the tithe. In this zone, we should feel very free to designate our preferences, whether within our local church or to other kingdom-building ministries.

> An expression of our gratitude to God. Have you ever written a thank-you note to God? It's as simple as expressing thank-you thoughts to him while you're writing your tithe check. This is the time to practice what the great hymn declares: "Count your blessings, name them one by one…" While I realize that we all have a gripe list, we should also all have a gratitude list. When you tithe, it's a time to express thanks for all the things on your gratitude list!

> An acknowledgment that everything we have was given to us by God (Deuteronomy 8:18). Who gives you the breath of life? Who gives you a beating heart? Who gave you the talents and abilities to produce the income that you produce? Who gives you opportunities to produce that income? God does! We acknowledge a beautiful thing when we tithe. We acknowledge our absolute dependence on our creator and sustainer!

> The biblical prescription for turning our hearts wholeheartedly to the Lord (Matthew 6:21). Even if you're presently unable to tithe with the right motives, the right thing to do is to tithe anyway. My wife and I tithed obediently before we learned to tithe joyfully. We would have never learned to tithe joyfully had we not been willing to tithe obediently first. While the Bible has a lot to say about our motives when giving,

it doesn't excuse us from giving simply because our motives are wrong. Don't wait until you get all your motives right to begin. Otherwise, you'll never start. Go ahead and honor God off the top, while praying that he will teach you proper motives

> Tithe even if you don't have the right motives…

as you obey! You'll experience the reality of the biblical principle: your heart will soon follow wherever you put your money (Matthew 6:21).

> ❯ A habit. Tithing is such a habit that you tithe off the top, even if you're going to be out of town the Sunday after payday. If you get paid next Friday and are planning a weekend get-away, drop your tithe check by the church before you leave town. If the church office is closed, place your tithe check in an envelope and mail it to your church before you leave town. By doing so, you're communicating to yourself, your family, and to God that he really is first in your life. You're also getting God's money out of your account before you accidentally spend it!

The Demonstration of Fearless Faith

Ruthie and I made a commitment to begin tithing and giving offerings. The bottom line to our commitment was this hard-and-fast principle: if anybody gets paid, God gets paid, regardless of the consequences.

We've discovered that God is not interested in casual Christians. He wants committed Christians (Revelation 3: 15–16). Therefore, we signed a vow to demonstrate *truly* fearless faith. I encourage you to sign that same vow (the "Vow to Demonstrate Fearless Faith" is located in the appendix, on page 135), to follow through on your commitment, and never to look back. You'll be so glad you did!

Do you have fearless faith in God? Joshua did! And because of his faith, he was willing to make a commitment that made no sense to his human, finite mind—dropping his weapons and picking up a trumpet at Jericho. If you really have faith, you'll drop the very thing you think you need the most and depend on God's help to eliminate your enemy—debt.

A Key Principle:

If anybody gets paid, God gets paid.

chapter **4**

The Snowball Payoff Priority Plan

When Ruthie and I committed to conquer debt God's way, we were bringing in $200 per month less than we needed to meet our minimum financial obligations. Only three weeks after we made our vows to God, we had $300 more than we needed to meet our minimum obligations. After five months, we had $750 per month more than our minimum obligations.

How would you like to have an extra $750 per month? And this was all accomplished with the money we already made! Some have asked how this is possible. The answer is through rapid and aggressive debt-elimination. After you've signed the "Vow to Declare War on Debt" (page 133), you'll realize that these "extra" dollars are really not discretionary at all, as you've committed to use the money for total debt elimination. But you get the idea.

The plan found in this chapter is the very one we used to get such dramatic results. However, I must remind you that these strategies only work effectively over time for those who have made the previous commitments found in this book.

I've known people who've skipped the first portion of this book to hurry and get to the practical strategies here, and I have yet to see one of them really succeed at debt elimination. They just didn't realize the value of building their debt-elimination plan upon total commitment to the process and honoring God with the top of their income. If you haven't read the preceding chapters, go back now and read them. Make the commitments, and then you'll really be ready for this war!

What The World Says About Conquering Debt

Why is it that the world teaches that when paying off debt, you should eliminate your highest interest credit cards first? Because the world believes we have an interest problem.

Most of us do not primarily have an interest problem. We have a cash flow problem! It's not difficult to pay off even high interest loans if you have discretionary cash flow. But many Americans have a negative cash flow. They literally have less money coming in than they have going out. This problem must be corrected pronto!

Let me illustrate. Ruthie and I had two separate $4,000 debts. One was on a credit card that was charging us 18%. The other debt was from a debt-consolidation loan that was charging us 12%. I began to wonder which of these debts would be the wisest to pay off first, assuming I had just been given $4,000.

I asked several different people for advice on this issue, including a banker, a CPA, a financial planner, a popular consumer credit counseling organization, a lawyer, and an insurance agent. I was amazed that they all gave the same answer. I was consistently told to pay off the credit card first because it was charging me the most interest. While this answer makes sense on the surface, an in-depth look reveals some surprising information.

Why Interest Isn't Everything

Let me prove to you that there are other powerful factors at work besides interest. Would you rather pay 1% interest or 100% interest? Of course you would answer 1%. Let me ask you a similar question with the addition of one variable. Would you rather pay 1% interest on a trillion dollars or 100% on one dollar? The best answer is 100% on a dollar. This illustration proves that interest isn't necessarily our biggest problem.

It may not make sense to pay off high-interest loans first...

It's often the payoff balance that's the bigger problem. Payoff balance is certainly a factor to consider when determining debt payoff order.

There's yet another key variable to consider. Let me ask you a question to help you to discover it for yourself. Why will you spend more money in interest on your low-interest house loan than you will on your high-interest credit card (other than the size of the payoff balance)? The answer is, of course, time.

When paying off debt, therefore, you have to consider three things: interest, payoff balance, and time. The world typically recommends that we pay attention only to interest and ignore balance and time. Ruthie and I decided to do the exact opposite. Why would we do such a radical thing—the very opposite of what the experts recommended? It's very simple.

The Bible tells us in Isaiah 55:8–9, "For my thoughts are not your thoughts, neither are your ways my ways, as the heavens are higher than the earth, so are my ways higher than your ways and my thoughts than your thoughts." Furthermore, the first three chapters of 1 Corinthians share a common theme, namely, that the wisdom of this world is foolishness to God, and that the foolishness of this world is really wisdom in the sight of God.

The bottom line is that this world often teaches us things that are not true. These falsehoods may sometimes be intentional, but oftentimes, they're accidental. Either way, it really doesn't matter. We end up deceived and led astray by the world. More often than not, you can please God by simply looking at what the world is doing—and then doing the opposite! Of course, I'm not recommending that you should fix your gaze on the world,

 If you want to conquer debt, focus on the Word, not on the world...

since this might tempt you to be like the world. A much better strategy to please God is to gaze at his Word and simply obey it, whether it makes sense to our human, finite minds or not.

What is the Snowball Payoff Priority Plan?

Ruthie and I decided to test our "opposite theory" in the area of finances. Since the world was teaching us to pay attention to interest and to neglect payoff balance and time altogether, we decided to pay attention to payoff balance and time and to neglect interest altogether. In thinking about the differences between God's way and the world's way, we developed a strategy that we call the "Snowball Payoff Priority Plan." This plan is based upon a mathematical formula that helps you line up your debts in such a manner as to free up cash rapidly as you aggressively pay off your debts. There's no better way to free up positive cash flow fast. The formula is simple:

$$\frac{payoff\ balance}{\div\ minimum\ monthly\ payment} = "months\ left"$$

I realize that this number is not technically accurate, because we've ignored interest. However, this number does represent time in a fair manner. In other words, we are literally ignoring interest, and focusing on *payoff balance* and *time*—the exact opposite of what is commonly taught in our world.

Do you remember the two separate $4000 debts I mentioned above? If I paid off the highest interest rate first, I would have freed up the minimum monthly payment on that credit card. However, if I paid off the debt consolidation loan first, I would have freed up that entire minimum monthly payment. Here comes the kicker. The credit card minimum payment was around $96 per month. The debt-consolidation loan minimum payment was about $435 per month.

Which would you rather have, an extra $96 per month or an extra $435 per month? The answer is obvious. Of course, you don't create this kind of cash flow by focusing on the highest interest loans first. You create it by using the Snowball Payoff Priority Plan. And once you've begun to free up money, you can use that money to further your war on debt!

How To Make a Snowball

Now that we've looked at the *why*, let's look at the *how*. Here's a step-by-step guide for making this happen:

1] Fill in the "Debt List" worksheet found on page 137 of the appendix. Include the names of your creditors, the payoff balances, and the minimum monthly payments;

2] For each of your debts, divide the payoff balance by the minimum monthly payment. Write the answer in the "Months Left" column.

3] Reorganize your debts using the "Snowball Payoff Priority Plan" worksheet on page 139, progressing from the debt with the fewest "months left" at the top of the chart to the debt with the most "months left" at the bottom of the chart.

4] Pay minimum monthly payments on all debts—except the top one. Attack the top one passionately with every penny you can get your hands on.

5] Once the top debt is paid off, take this newly-available money and designate it as your "debt-elimination snowball." Add this amount to the minimum payment you're sending to the next creditor on the list. Continue to commit every penny you can to conquer this debt.

6] Continue in this fashion as each debt gets paid.

Below is a sample of a completed Snowball Payoff Priority Plan. Note that we've already organized these debts by "months left."

Creditor	Balance	"Months Left"	Minimum Payment	Snowball Amount
Credit Union	$300.00	3.00	$100.00	$100.00
First National	$728.00	5.00	$153.00	$253.00
Grandmom	$1,200.00	12.00	$100.00	$353.00
J.C. Penney	$218.00	12.11	$18.00	$371.00
Orthodontist	$1,300.00	13.00	$100.00	$471.00
Visa #1	$530.00	34.00	$16.00	$487.00
Dillards	$965.00	39.00	$25.00	$512.00
Car	$12,821.00	43.00	$299.00	$811.00
Visa #2	$2,913.00	50.22	$58.00	$869.00
Mastercard	$4,800.00	50.53	$95.00	$964.00
House Mortgage	$72,000.00	96.00	$750.00	$1,714.00

Using the Snowball Payoff Priority Plan will knock years off the time it takes you to eliminate debt, and it will save you thousands of dollars in the process.

Momentum Money: Fighting with Every Resource

In addition to using our "debt-elimination snowball," Ruthie and I minimized every regular expense we could. We cut cable television, which freed up $40 per month, which of course we added to the snowball. We cut our grocery bill *in half*. We minimized the money we were spending on clothes, and so forth. These sacrifices greatly accelerated the process of conquering debt.

We strongly encourage you to make similar sacrifices. Realize that any sacrifices you make now are not permanent! We now have cable television again. However, when you're at war, much sacrifice is required. When you've won the war and are back in the land of peace, you can and will enjoy great blessings!

We recommend that you find 5% of your income through sacrificial cutbacks to accelerate this entire process. We refer to this amount as Momentum Money! Once you find this money, you simply add it to the minimum payment of your first debt. Continue to leave this money in the Debt-Elimination Snowball until all your debt is paid!

Defeating the "Miscellaneous Monster"

You may be thinking, "There's no way I can find 5% of my income to accelerate the process." We'd like to ask, why not? You might say, "Because in the previous chapter, you 10-percented me, then you 2-percented me, then you Holy Spirit-percented me, and now you're 5-percenting me. I just don't have that much money available. In fact, I'm already short of meeting minimum financial obligations." I have great news for you. The average American family loses up to 30% of their income to the "miscellaneous monster." If you can kill this monster, you'll have enough money to do everything we've described above and still have money left over for pizza and a movie.

> The average American family loses up to 30% of their income to miscellaneous expenses.

I want to give you one more challenge before describing this next strategy. Make debt elimination your second financial priority each month! In other words, pay God first, pay all your debts second (even if you're halfway down your debt list, continue to use the total snowball payment toward your debts), and then use the remainder to meet your needs.

Putting Yourself and Your Budget on a Diet

I'll never forget an experience we had after deciding to adopt these priorities. Ruthie came to me and announced, "We have a problem. We have no food and no money. But at least God got paid, and the debts got paid. I hope you're happy!"

After further investigation, we discovered that we did have some food—it just wasn't food we liked. We were confronted with a tough choice. We could either eat the food we had but didn't like, or we could compromise our commitment to God and purchase food we liked using a credit card. We decided we would keep our commitment regardless of the cost. We ate "yucky" food until the next payday (about a week).

As a result of this experience, the next month we became some of the smartest shoppers in Lubbock County! We paid attention when we shopped. We bought "FakeOs" instead of Cheerios™ ("FakeOs" are an off-brand Cheerios™ that taste stale. They're sold under the names of "TastyOs," "NastiOs," and "YuckiOs." Though they do not initially taste as good as the real thing, we got used to them after awhile). We used coupons. We looked for sales. We developed a menu, made a list, and stuck to the list when shopping. We would have never learned to minimize living expenses unless we followed the God-first/debt-second priority.

Learning from Mistakes

Our story isn't just full of successes. We've failed along the way as well. Some of the most valuable lessons we learned came from failure. One such occasion occurred about two years into the process. After eliminating all of our debt except our mortgage, I decided we should change our financial priorities. I decided to continue to pay God first, but then to take care of our needs second, and then to throw the leftover money on top of our mortgage.

If you look at the chart on page 68, you'll notice that this meant putting the minimum payment on our house ($750 per month) and leaving the rest of the $964 in our snowball in the bank for "needs." At the end of the month, we planned to take whatever was left from this $964 and add it to the principle of our house. Guess how much was left over? Absolutely *nothing*. I convinced myself that this was no big deal. After all, we had been sacrificing for a long time, and we probably had legitimate needs that ate up that money. We continued in this pattern for an entire year. There was not a single occasion when we had even a dime left over to apply to the principle of our mortgage. And yet, when it was all said and done,

> Keep your priorities clear: it's too easy to sacrifice extra money in your account to the "miscellaneous monster!"

we also had nothing to show for this missing money and couldn't even recall how we had spent it.

We were able to determine that we shopped differently when we had an extra $964 sitting around in our bank account. It's just so easy to buy more things, better things, and often unnecessary things when the money is in the bank. We learned that we didn't want money sitting around in the bank. We needed to get it out of our bank account and toward our debt quickly—otherwise, the "miscellaneous monster" would eat it!

This principle is taught clearly by Stephen Covey in his bestseller, *The Seven Habits of Highly Effective People*. He takes some big rocks, some pebbles, and some sand and demonstrates how all these ingredients will fit into a clear fishbowl as long as they are placed into the fishbowl in the following order—big rocks first, pebbles second, and sand third. However, these same ingredients won't fit into the fishbowl if you place them in the fishbowl in any other order, an example that works in our financial lives as well.

Your paycheck will likely be able to fund everything so long as you pay God first, debts second, and needs third. But, if you change this order, something won't get paid.

chapter **5**

Be Disciplined in Your Efforts (Part 1)

In the previous chapter, we explored the idea of building a "snowball," using the money freed up from paying off one debt to work towards paying off other debts. But this isn't the only weapon you have in your arsenal. As I pointed out, you could also trim your grocery budget in order to use the extra "momentum money" to help reduce your debt even further.

In this chapter and the next one, I'll show you even more ways of building momentum in your battle against debt. However, these strategies are not only important for their economic benefit, but also because they'll help discipline you for your battle. Remember: even with God's help, Joshua and the Isrealites had to fight for a long time to conquer the land. Your fight with debt may take a long time, too, but if you maintain your discipline, you'll be able to follow through and be victorious!

Sell Stuff!

If you could sell some stuff, you could use this money to further accelerate the process. We did this in several ways. First of all, we had several garage sales. Our first sale brought in $1000. Do you want to know a guaranteed method of making $1000 in a garage sale? Sell 4000 things at a quarter each! I'm attempting

> Minimize the everyday expenses of life; maximize the money you put toward debt.

to show you a powerful lesson: big money often comes from

Big money can come from selling lots of things for "small money."

small money happening over and over again. We didn't make $1000 by having nice, valuable stuff. We made the $1000 by selling lots and lots of little stuff!

Sandra Felton has written a book entitled *The Messies Manual*. In this highly-recommended book, she describes two types of people; Messies and Cleanies. Below is my oversimplified explanation of this relevant subject.

"Messies" are pack rats, clutter bugs, stuff accumulators. "Cleanies" feel claustrophobic in the presence of lots of stuff.

If you go to Messies' homes and look in their garages, you won't find cars there. Messies don't have room for cars in their garages. Instead, their garages are full of stuff. If you go to Cleanies' homes and look in their garages, you'll find 2 cars and 1 broom (which is hanging neatly on the wall).

In God's great sense of humor, he usually leads a Messie to marry a Cleanie. This results in a lifelong conflict of one spouse bringing truckloads of stuff home, while the other spouse discards it behind his or her back.

My wife and I have never experienced this particular marriage struggle because we are both Messies! We decided we would work at being pack rats together, accumulating clutter and stuff.

But God convicted us that we were too stuff-focused. He told us to sell our stuff.

Those of you who are Messies know that the last thing Messies want to hear is that they should sell their stuff. For Messies, there's a strange sense of emotional security that comes from stuff. While this isn't healthy, it *is* a reality.

I argued with God about whether or not to sell our stuff. And God had a more difficult time convincing me to sell my stuff than he did convincing me to tithe. You have to be a Messie to understand.

A typical Messie responds by saying, "I can't sell my stuff. I might need it someday!" To this, God says, "Risk it—maybe you won't need it. And if you later need something you sold, I'll help you cross that bridge when you get there." After recalling our commitment to obey God regardless of whether it made sense or not, Ruthie and I succumbed.

We estimate that we sold around 20,000 items. After doing so, we discovered that we really only missed one thing. Is it possible that Messies are holding on to numerous things for fear they may need them someday, when in fact they might only miss one thing? Absolutely!

> It's not a tragedy to sell something you need later; it's a tragedy to hang onto 19,999 things you'll never need.

The one thing we later needed was a coffee pot. We owned three coffee pots and sold all three. Though we missed the coffee pot, God taught us some valuable lessons as a result. For example, I learned that there are many places in town where you can find free coffee! I also learned that I can survive without coffee, and I learned that I could replace the coffee pot with proceeds from the garage sale if I wanted to. The moral of the story is: it's just not that tragic if you sell something that you later need!

Go ahead and sell your stuff. Risk it! We were surprised to discover that we enjoyed life more after getting rid of stuff. The stuff that we thought was a blessing was actually a burden. But we didn't even realize it until we had the courage to get rid of it.

And we quickly used the money from the sale of stuff to throw toward our top-listed unpaid debt. As we successfully paid off debt, we began to realize that there are some things in life that are better than stuff—such as extra money at the end of every month!

After our first garage sale, we had two subsequent sales. We reduced the prices and made $500 from one and $250 from the other, adding up to $1750 from garage sales in only 3 weeks (you'll want to check your city ordinances before having 3 consecutive weeks of garage sales; it's actually against the law in some places).

In addition to garage sales, we also separately sold our bigger and better items. There are some things we had that would bring better money if advertised separately. Some of the items we sold included: a computer ($100), a guitar ($300), a china cabinet ($250), a camera ($50), baseball cards ($450), and sets of magic tricks ($125). These items added up to $1275. This added up to a grand total of around $3000, including the garage sales.

What did we do with $3000? You know the answer by now! We attacked debt quickly. It's a mistake to let this money sit around in your bank account for a month. Get it toward

 Don't let extra money sit in your bank account, or the "miscellaneous monster" will eat it!

your debt *immediately*. If you don't, the Miscellaneous Monster will eat it! This $3000 enabled us to pay off the top 5 debts on our Snowball plan and free up $471 per month in positive cash flow.

What would have happened if we had applied this $3000 to the highest interest credit card first (the Mastercard in the table on page 68)? We would have paid off zero debts and created very little cash flow (since the minimum payment would have dropped by only about $55 per month).

Again, which would you rather have? Five debts paid off and significant positive cash flow or zero debts paid off and very little positive cash flow? You can get either one for the same $3000 investment. How did we go from $200 short each month to $300 long each month? By selling stuff and paying off debt according to the Snowball Payoff Priority Plan.

If you're renting a storage building to store stuff, you could sell the stuff and put that money toward your debt. Then you'd also no longer need to rent the storage building, freeing up the rental fee each month to add to your debt-reduction snowball.

However, as you work through this process, be aware that procrastination will raise its ugly head and offer you several reasons why you can't go to all this trouble right now. It seems that some value the doctrine of procrastination right alongside the doctrines of the priesthood of all believers and the preservation of the saints. Don't be one of them or you'll never get out of debt!

Also be aware that the stuff you're selling will have drastically dropped in value. The baseball cards that I sold for $475 cost me over $5000. You must be emotionally prepared for this, or you'll be tempted to keep your stuff. The last thing you need is stuff left over to place back in the attic! You need positive cash flow. And you get there much faster by selling lots of stuff—even at drastically depreciated prices!

Discover the Benefits of Clutter-Free Living

Ruthie and I were having another problem during this time in our lives. After a particularly moving sermon from our pastor, we became convicted that God wanted us to become more hospitable. Though we are not "gifted" in hospitality, we are called by God to be hospitable (as is every believer). But being Messies, we went into panic mode every time the doorbell rang unexpectedly.

It was so bad that we had to train our daughters in a game that we called "Dash and Stash." It's next to impossible to have an ongoing attitude of hospitality when there's constantly a mess around the house.

In an effort to solve this crisis, we enrolled in a class called "Speed Cleaning." The first rule of speed cleaning is to get rid of your clutter. Though we had already sold much of our stuff, this motivated us to reduce our stuff even further. As we continued to downsize, we learned that clutter carries with it a very high price, which involves time costs, space costs, energy costs, financial costs, and worry costs.

Time Costs...

I've always been fascinated with the subject of time-management. I've been to many seminars on the subject and carry a day planner with a calendar and to-do list. However, the best time management principle I ever learned didn't come from a seminar. I learned it by accident as we downsized our stuff.

The principle is this: the more stuff you have, the less time you have. Conversely, the less stuff you have, the more time you have.

Let's assume that you're an internet junkie. You enjoy coming home from work, sitting down at the computer, and exploring the World Wide Web. What would happen if you sold the computer and canceled your subscription with your internet service provider? In addition to finding money to apply to your debt, you'd now come home after work and have more discretionary time on your hands.

A Surprising Fact:

The more stuff you have, the less time you have. The less stuff you have, the more time you have...

I'm not recommending that you sell your computer — though I did. I'm simply illustrating that new discretionary time becomes available when you get rid of stuff.

Space Costs...

Stuff takes up lots of space. I remember being frustrated because every time I played with my daughters on the floor of our living room, I would hit my head on the coffee table or the end table. During a quiet time with God one morning, I expressed this frustration by requesting a better salary so I could purchase a bigger home with more space in the living room. God answered my prayer. He said, "You don't need more space. You need to sell the coffee table and the end table." We did. I haven't hit my head on them since.

If we'll be truthful with ourselves, we'll realize that we can't afford the cost of having a home full of clutter. The clutter in our lives will drain us spiritually, mentally, physically, and financially. For those of us who have children, having a home full of clutter teaches them that things are a high priority and encourages them to have a materialistic mindset. We can't afford junk! It's time to de-junk our homes and de-clutter our lives!

"Where do we start?" you ask. Pick a closet, cabinet, or drawer and take everything out of it. Then, sort or try on everything and place each thing in one of the boxes you have ready. You'll need a box each for trash, garage sale items, things to be fixed or mended, things you've borrowed and need to return, things that belong elsewhere in the house, and things that you need to keep. You may need more categories. We agreed that if we hadn't used anything in a year, it went out (unless it had significant sentimental value). Be strong! And if some item of clothing doesn't fit or it doesn't flatter you, out it goes! If you lose weight, you can buy new clothes later!

When we got to the kitchen, we discovered that we owned multiples of many items, and so we kept only the ones we really liked, needed, and used. We did the same thing in each room of the house.

We encouraged our girls to de-clutter, too, by allowing them to put their old items in our garage sale and by allowing them to keep the money their items brought in. We also put the toys they wanted to keep in plastic storage boxes; if the boxes are full when they get a new toy, they have to get rid of an old one to make room for the new one.

Sometimes our walls can get cluttered, too. Take a look at your walls as if you were a visitor to your home. Do you notice the things that are most important to you, or do they get lost in the clutter? We discovered that we wanted fewer things — keeping only those that we really liked.

All of this has led us to an important conclusion: we now think the best look for a home is "clean and clutter-free!" And we've realized something else important, too: the average American family doesn't need a bigger house; they just need *less stuff*.

 The average American family doesn't need a bigger home; they just need less stuff!

Energy Costs...

One of the greatest costs of having stuff is energy. The truth of the matter is, the more stuff you have, the less energy you have. The less stuff you have, the more energy you have.

Ruthie and I used to have an ongoing battle about my shoes. I would consistently kick them off all around the house. This drove her crazy. She'd ask me to pick up my shoes, but I never would. The reason? I was always out of energy.

This never happens now because I sold all my shoes except for two pairs. I kept a pair of burgundy wing tips and a pair of tennis shoes. I told Ruthie I wanted wing tips because they never go out of style. She told me they were never in style! I chose burgundy, since that color goes with almost anything.

Whenever I wear khakis or nicer on the dress scale, I wear burgundy wing tips. Whenever I wear jeans or down on the dress scale, I wear tennis shoes. I have no other options.

Now when Ruthie asks me to pick up my shoes, I'm glad to do it because it doesn't take much energy to pick up two pairs of shoes. In addition, I now have plenty of energy. I have more energy now than I had when I was 25. The reason: I drastically downsized my stuff. Stuff is always a drain on one's energy.

Money Costs...

It takes money to have clutter. It requires money to buy it, to insure it, to maintain it, to repair it, and to clean it. The more stuff you have, the less money you have. The reverse is also true!

Worry Costs...

I used to worry about my baseball card collection each time my family and I left town. I was worried that someone might break into our house and steal it. Do you know how hard it is to enjoy a vacation when you're constantly worried that your prized possession might be snatched? It's impossible.

I don't have that problem anymore. When we leave town, I don't worry. If someone breaks into our house, there's no stuff that we really obsess or worry or care about left to steal!

The Benefits...

Do you think God wants you to use some of your greatest resources like time, space, energy, and money to be relationship-focused or to be stuff-focused?

God has a people purpose, not a stuff purpose, for each one of us! Even if you're an introvert, God has a people purpose for you. While introverts will sometimes need to withdraw from the crowds to reenergize, they must then launch back out into people groups to serve them in the name of Jesus Christ. The bottom line to this discussion is that the more stuff you have, the less time, space, energy, and money you have—and the more worry you have. The less stuff you have, the more time, space, energy, and money you have—and less worry!

Jesus said everything I've just said to you. In Luke 12:15, Jesus says, "Watch out! Be on your guard against all kinds of greed; a man's life does not consist in the abundance of his stuff" (okay, a slight paraphrase).

This is the second key mentioned in this book for discovering life—true, abundant, meaningful, significant life. In Chapter 3, we discovered that true life is reserved for those who are willing to be generous. Now we discover that true life is also reserved for those who are not stuff-focused. Get rid of your stuff! Then go looking for true life. You'll find it in your relationships with God and others—and you'll be released from the burden of stuff addiction.

Two Keys for Discovering True Life
1] Tithe regularly and give offerings.
2] Get rid of stuff!

Most people fail to go far enough with getting rid of stuff. I encourage people to go further with this concept than they have ever imagined. Ruthie and I actually went so far as to sell things that we regularly used. "Like what?" you ask. Like our dining room table and chairs. Where did we eat? On the floor!

A dining room table and chairs is not a *need*. No one has ever died for lack of a dining room table and chairs. In fact, the majority of people alive today have never had a dining room table and chairs. Of course, the Bible records Jesus Christ himself as having eaten while reclining on the floor. The absence of a dining room table and chairs was a daily reminder that we were no longer in the land of peace. We were at war. It's critical to keep this mindset throughout the entire debt-elimination process because this focus leads to success.

I'm not recommending that you get rid of your dining room table and chairs. But I *am* recommending that you go further with the idea of downsizing than you would have ever previously considered. Going as far as you can will create extra cash with which you can attack debt. It also helps you to become less stuff-focused and addicted.

By the way, we now own a wonderful dining room table and chairs. When I ask you to consider making sacrifices, I want you to know that these are not permanent—they're tempo-

Sacrificing stuff doesn't have to be permanent, but it can bring great benefits and can help you refocus your priorities.

rary. Remember to keep your focus on the benefits of having no debt, rather than on the sacrifices you must endure to arrive there.

Let me give you a few warnings to prevent you from going too far. Be careful not to get rid of something that has great sentimental value (though it's also wrong to attach sentimental value to everything just so you can keep it all). Don't sell something that you're unwilling to live without for an extended period of time. And don't push your spouse to sell something he or she is unwilling to sell.

Follow a Spending Plan

In addition to selling stuff, we decided to follow a spending plan. That way, we could plan for future expenses and track what we were spending. In making our plan, we developed a 3-account budgeting process, which is depicted in the following table. You'll notice that we have Bank Account 1, Bank Account 2, and a Cash Expenses Box.

	Income		
	Bank Account 1	**Bank Account 2**	**Cash Expenses Box**
Type	Standard checking account	Standard checking account	"Envelope system"
Purpose	Paying tithing, debts, utilities and immediate needs	Paying long-term or irregular fees and upcoming needs	Paying living and miscellaneous expenses
Examples	Tithes and offerings, credit card debts, mortgage, auto gasoline, telephone bills, electric bills, etc.	Car insurance, life and health insurance, income tax, birthday and Christmas gifts, auto repair, etc.	Groceries, dates, clothes, haircuts, entertainment and eating out, etc.
Balances	Spend to zero every month	Always keep a balance	Spend as needed, but only after careful thought and prayer

These accounts have different purposes. Account 1 is for regular monthly expenses that are hard to pay cash for and that have a low temptation factor. For example, notice that utility bills are covered by this account. My utility companies want money each month. These bills are also difficult to pay in cash—doable, but inconvenient because of the amounts involved. And finally my utility companies have a low temptation factor. In other words, we've never been tempted to send our utility companies extra money. This just isn't one of our sin tendencies.

Account 2 is for upcoming needs. These aren't monthly items, but they're still things we must prepare for in order to prevent the need for a credit card in the future. For example, as we said earlier, we put $50 per month in this account for Christmas gifts. After doing so for twelve months, we were able to withdraw $600 in cash for our Christmas shopping.

Had we not done this, we would have had to turn to credit cards for gift purchasing.

The "Cash Expenses Box" is a simple revision of the tried-and-true "envelope system." We purchased a small plastic box from an office supply store that was designed to file 4" × 6" note cards. Then, Ruthie took some manila folders and cut them down to fit in this box and we wrote different cash categories on the tabs. At each payday, we distribute a portion of my salary into each of the folders. When we shop for groceries, for example, we take money from the grocery folder and make our purchases. We place any change

Keep cash on hand for living expenses and optional expenses. When you run out of cash, quit spending!

back in the folder and return it to the Cash Expenses Box upon returning home. The Cash Expenses Box encourages us to be careful with our budget, because when we run out of money in a category, we stop spending.

The secret to this whole system is that we never "rob Peter to pay Paul." We pay for nothing out of Account 1 except those items listed there. We pay for nothing out of Account 2 except those items listed there. And we never take cash out of the clothes envelope and to go see a movie. Why? Because we have a dating category for that. While we don't date outside the marriage, we do date within our marriage! And some of the things we enjoy doing require money. But when

Stay disciplined! Never use money from one category to pay for items in another category...

the money in the dating folder is gone, we stop going out until the next payday when new money is placed in this folder (or we go on a walk together for free).

Ruthie and I tried the envelope system for years with no success. But after we signed the "Vow to Declare War on Debt" (see page 133), we became immediately successful. Before signing the vow, we used to "rob Peter to pay Paul" often. But after signing the vow to God, we were no longer comfortable making compromises. The secret to your success is in your commitment, not in the system! You can get out of debt with a bad system if you're committed. But, you can also remain in debt with a great system if you're *not* committed. Rapid debt elimination occurs when you combine commitment with an incredible system. This is the "Conquering Debt God's Way" approach.

To make your plan work, you'll need to write your spending down somewhere. You should record your income plus the amount you need for your tithes, your debt reduction, and your bills, in addition to any other spending. Ruthie and I have ours written on a piece of notebook paper. If you prefer, you can use the various worksheets that we've included in the appendix on pages 141–151. How do you develop a spending plan? Here's a step-by-step guide :

1] Calculate your total income, being sure to include your salaries and any regular income from investments;

2] Create appropriate categories for all of your expenses. In doing this, it may be useful to consult the list of sample categories that appears in the appendix on page 143.

3] Set amounts for each of the entries on your spending plan. Some, like your tithe, you can calculate directly from your income. For others, like utility bills, it may be helpful to save old bills or look over amounts you've paid previously so you can calculate an average. In addition, some utility companies will spread out payments so you pay a standard amount each month. It may be helpful for budgeting purposes to check into such arrangements since it will make your payments more consistent.

4] Since rapid debt elimination is your primary financial objective, make your spending plan as bare-bones as possible. Remember that this is only temporary, and the more you can successfully cut back now, the sooner you'll be debt free. We'd also recommend that you find at least 5% of your income to accelerate your debt reduction. This "momentum money" will remind you about your commitment and will help you to be disciplined in your efforts.

5] Make sure your expenses fit in your income. If they don't, find areas to cut back and make necessary adjustments. If you discover that you need to sacrifice something, don't sacrifice God's portion or the portion committed to debt reduction. Choose a portion of your own expenses to sacrifice instead.

6] It's important to keep track of how you're spending your money. We recommend using a record-keeping system that's simple. The method we've used is as follows: since Account 1 and Account 2 are regular checking accounts, we keep records of our expenses in the ledgers for those accounts. For the cash expenses box, we simply put the amount of cash we've allotted for each category in the appropriate envelope. As long as there's money in that envelope, we know we can still make purchases.

7] Once you've established it, live by your spending plan! This whole system will be worthless if you make purchases impulsively. When an account or an envelope is empty, you can no longer spend money in that category until you're able to replenish the money the following month. *Never* take money from the clothes envelope to go to the movies—even if you intend to replace it the next month from your entertainment fund. When you've spent all the money in that category, you're done. This may seem binding at first, but in time, you'll see that it's actually freeing.

8] Leave the house daily with no money, no credit cards, and no checkbook. The only exception is when you leave the house with a purpose that fits into your spending plan.

9] Set a time and a place where you regularly meet to review your spending plan, to pay bills, and to pray about and discuss conquering debt. If you're married, do this with your spouse!

Following these nine steps will help you make the most of your efforts to eliminate your debt. Remember the three most important principles of this plan: 1) pay bills weekly—and if you're married, work together; 2) pay God first, debt second, and then live off of what's left; and 3) when you run out of money in one category, *stop spending*. If you'd like some additional help with budgeting, resources by such authors as Larry Burkett, Ron Blue, Dave Ramsey, and Mary Hunt are available at your Christian bookstores.

Basic Principles

1] Pay bills together weekly;
2] Pay God first, debt second, and live off of the rest;
3] When you run out of money in one category, stop spending.

Consider Postponing Retirement Savings

We decided to stop putting money aside for retirement—temporarily. Instead, we placed that money in the Debt-Elimination Snowball.

You may ask, "What are you going to do about retirement?" It has something to do with having an extra $1714 per month that comes once you've paid off your debts! When you're completely debt-free, you can turn your Debt-Elimination Snowball into a "Rapid-Retirement Snowball!"

If you save this $1714 per month for 25 years and average a 12% return on your money, you'll have three and a quarter million dollars set aside for retirement. I think you could retire on that! If you could save it for 30 years at 12%, you'd have $6 million. I'm pretty sure you could retire even better on that!

Postponing your retirement savings is not necessarily bad, especially if you're totally committed to rapid debt elimination and committed to using

Your retirement fund will thrive in a debt-free environment.

your newly freed-up money to reach your God-directed retirement goals.

In reality, it isn't likely that you'll be able to save your entire snowball for retirement, as you may need to put a portion of it aside for other future financial needs. And, as we've already discussed, you may want to greatly increase your giving to God. Ruthie and I have 3 daughters and therefore need to save up for weddings and college education. We need to be putting money aside for a vehicle replacement fund. We want to create some special family memories with our girls before they leave home and are therefore saving for some special activities. A small lifestyle upgrade may also be acceptable with a portion of your snowball. These kinds of things are valid; however, you should give retirement planning a high priority the very second you become debt-free.

There is an exception to the above. If you work for a company that offers you a "matching funds" retirement option, I think you should sign on immediately with the highest contribution they will match. You cannot afford *not* to be involved in such a great opportunity.

Consider Using Accumulated Savings

Ruthie and I withdrew $1,250 from one retirement fund and $2,850 from another retirement fund to use for debt elimination. By doing so, we were penalized to the tune of 10% by the IRS for early withdrawal. In addition, the

IRS added these amounts into our taxable salary for the year. This meant we had to pay a bigger percentage on a bigger salary, plus suffer the 10% early withdrawal penalty. Thus, I hesitate even to mention the idea of withdrawing retirement money to you, as it often doesn't make sense. However, I feel an obligation to share this strategy with you, as this is one of the key strategies we used to transition from $200 short each month to $750 long each month in only five months.

Of course, you may have money sitting in savings vehicles, which are unrelated to retirement and would have no negative tax implications if withdrawn. It often makes sense to withdraw these. It makes no sense to me to have money in the bank drawing 4% interest (and that's often optimistic) when you're paying 18% on a credit card (which is more like 96% interest as we've seen if you're paying minimum payments each month). While withdrawing savings is not often recommended by accountants, it made sense for us. Let me show you why.

> Make 4% interest on savings or save 96% by not owing interest on credit card debt? You decide...

This withdrawal, along with the sale of stuff and sacrificial lifestyle cutbacks, resulted in raising our snowball to $750 per month. This was such a sizable amount that we could have used it to repay the money we had just "robbed" from our retirement account in only six months. In doing so, we would also have been able to make up for the penalties and lost interest, and we would still be left with a $750 snowball when the six-month payback of our retirement fund was completed (though we didn't use the money to replace our retirement—we used it for further debt elimination, knowing that we would replace our retirement fund after we had eliminated all our debt).

Of course, this strategy only makes sense if you're withdrawing a relatively small amount of money (we withdrew around $4000) and you are able to free up a large amount of money (we freed up $750 per month).

I ran into a schoolteacher once who told me she had three debts: house ($500 per month), car ($200 per month), and lawyer ($50 per month). She went on to say that she had $45,000 in a Teacher Retirement fund and another $35,000 in an IRA. She said that she could eliminate all her debt if she withdrew this $80,000 from retirement funds. She then asked for my opinion.

I said, "No way!" Her 10% early withdrawal penalty would have cost her $8000 right off the top. Then the IRS would have added $80,000 to her salary for the year. This would have turned her $30,000 teaching salary into $110,000. The income taxes on such a large amount would be frightening!

Withdrawal didn't make sense for her situation as she was dealing with huge money in order to free up small money. It would have taken her many years of using her freed-up snowball money to replace what she had withdrawn. Her situation was thus very different than ours.

Consider a Part-Time Job

Though the debt-reduction system we've described here is workable with just the money you presently make, additional income applied toward debt can accelerate the process.

Back when I was a full-time associate pastor in a local church setting, I was confronted by a minister who said, "Our church is going to have a Valentine's banquet for senior adults. We're looking for someone to wash dishes following the banquet. Do you have anybody in your church who needs to make a little extra money?" I immediately volunteered for the job. This caught him by surprise, so he reminded me that it only paid minimum wage and that it would rob me of the opportunity to take my wife out for a Valentine's dinner. I accepted the job anyway. Then I called my wife and said, "Ruthie, Valentine's Day is coming up and I thought we might want to do something together." I went on to tell her about the opportunity we had to wash dishes that night.

There's no way I can express the importance of spouses being in this war together. My wife could have threatened me, accused me of loving debt-elimination more than I loved her, or even slapped me. She didn't. Instead, she said something like this, "Bruce, I knew when we signed the vow to eliminate debt that we were leaving the land of peace and entering the land of warfare. Though I didn't fully understand the implications of that decision then, I knew that sacrifice would be the name of the game. Count me in!" We made a total of $28 that night.

By the way, we did go out for lunch that day—and discovered that we didn't have to stand in line for two hours like the evening crowd did. The lunch menu was also less expensive.

Let me ask you two questions. First, is there any amount of money that's so small that you would be unwilling to work for it? I've worked in paying jobs since I was 10 years old. I had always made more than minimum wage until the dishwashing job. I was honestly tempted to skip the job because it didn't pay enough. But that would have been a big mistake. One valuable lesson that I learned was that the big money is in the small money (when you can get it to repeat itself). Think about it. If I could have talked that church into hiring me to do the same job a million times, I would have made $28 million! Don't let small money opportunities discourage you.

You can make big money from small change — if it repeats...

Second, is there any job that you consider beneath you? If so, you have a bigger problem than a debt problem! You have a pride problem. And a pride problem is a big problem.

I had previously considered myself "too good" to wash dishes. After all, I was a white-collar professional. But God led me to James 4:6 where the Bible says, "God opposes the proud, but gives grace to the humble." Similarly, in Proverbs, God reminds us, "Pride goes before a fall." When pursuing total debt elimination, the last thing I needed was God's opposition—for God himself to stick out his foot and trip me. I humbled myself and washed the dishes.

You can be a born-again believer in Jesus Christ, and on your way to heaven when you die, and still be opposed by God in the present. Think back to the story of Joshua. In chapter seven, we find a most surprising occurrence. God actually helps the enemy to defeat his own children. This occurred at a place called Ai and resulted from Achan's obsession with stuff (sound familiar?). We must be careful to obey God's teachings. And one of his most importance teachings is to be humble!

In his book *Experiencing God*, Henry Blackaby says, "Humble yourself or God will humiliate you." If God asks you to take a job that you previously considered beneath you, take it quickly. In addition to extra money to add to your snowball, you'll prove to yourself, your family, the world, and to God that you want to be a humble person.

In addition to washing dishes, my wife also took a part-time preschool job at our church. Though my wife is a certified school teacher by profession, she wanted to stay home with our children once they were born. But even with her goal to be a stay-at-home mom, she was able to produce some income. She started making around $185 per month working only 6 hours per week. She could have said, "This is my miscellaneous money," but she didn't. She wanted to add this to our snowball. Her contributions made a huge impact on our success.

We also started cleaning houses. Remember—I was a full-time associate pastor during this time in our lives. I had an 8-to-5 job already. I also had to be available for church emergencies 24 hours per day. Yet even with these demands, I found time to clean houses.

We asked a local real estate agent if they ever hired people to clean vacant homes. They informed us that they did. We started to bid some of these jobs and got several of them. Since the homes were vacant, we were able to clean them any time of day. I remember getting up long before my church job and cleaning houses. When I went to work at church, Ruthie would go over to the house and continue the cleaning job. We would often meet at the house and split an 80¢ sack lunch. I would also clean after my office hours if needed.

Ruthie would babysit occasionally. $10 here and $25 there added up in a hurry. I started a lawn care business named "Mr. Mow-it-All." I was still a full-time minister at the time, but my church gave me two days off each week—Saturdays and Mondays. I tried to make Saturdays a family day and Mondays a mowing day. After tithe, taxes, and legitimate business expenses, I made around $3500, which we promptly threw toward our mortgage. This "little money" paid off over 5 years of a 30-year mortgage.

I have one warning for you regarding part-time jobs, however. There are many things in life that are more important than debt elimination. One of those is your family life. If you're married, you have relationship responsibilities toward your spouse. If you're a parent, you have relationship responsibilities toward your children. You also have commitments to God and his church through committed attendance and volunteer service. Don't become so obsessed with extra work opportunities that you fail in these considerably more important areas of life!

Say No to Shortcuts and Magic Pills

Sometimes, the longest distance between two points is a shortcut! Shortcuts don't always pay off in the long run.

I ran into an old friend some time ago, who commented, "You've lost weight; you look great. How did you do it?" I responded, "I've started eating right and exercising." My friend replied, "Yuck, I don't want to do that." I asked, "What do you want to do?" He responded, "I really hoped you had a magic pill that you could sell me that would melt the fat off my body with no pain or effort on my part."

This friend perfectly describes most Americans. Our culture is looking for an easy, pain-free way to solve whatever problems we may be facing. Yet you must stand strong against this kind of mentality. This mentality by itself will keep you in debt. As long as you believe that there's hope of winning the lottery or hitting it big in a get-rich-quick scheme, you won't really commit yourself to the sacrifices necessary to become debt-free.

> As long as you believe there's hope of getting out of debt the easy way, you won't really succeed...

I know of several people who rejected the principles in this book, and opted instead for get-rich-quick opportunities. They didn't get rich, and they're now deeper in debt than ever!

Though I've played the lottery in the past, God convicted me to stop after signing the "Vow to Demonstrate Fearless Faith" (page 135). After all, whom was I trusting—God or the lottery? Ruthie and I decided that either God would help us to get out of debt, or we would just have to stay in debt. We have never regretted that decision!

Assume for a moment that you were to win the lottery. Several things would likely result. First, it would ruin many of your relationships with people you love. I once saw a television program featuring eight people who had won the lottery. Each of them deeply regretted the wonderful relationships that were destroyed due to envy, loans that weren't repaid, etc. *All eight* desired to have their old lives back and wished they hadn't won! Second, it would ruin your character. Your motivation to work would be snatched away. Lottery winners often live their lives like spoiled brats. Their character is often changed. Third, you'd be consumed by excessive materialism. Why do many play the lottery in the first place? Because of greed! Greed is a sin. If you win, you feed your sinful nature. Fourth, if you play the lottery, you *won't* win! You have a better chance of being struck by lightning—twice!—than of winning the lottery! Fifth, who gets the glory for your debt elimination success? The lottery, luck, the state? It's common for a lottery winner's testimony to be used as radio commercials to seduce others into playing. God never intended for you to use the incredible power of your testimony to lead others into sin. He wants you to reserve the incredible power of your testimony to give glory to him and to point others to him.

Ironically, many who win the lottery find their lives destroyed by their new wealth.

We've seen God honored and others come to saving faith in Jesus as a result of our testimony. The reason is that we conquered debt God's way, not the lottery way! The sooner you run from financial shortcuts (as Proverbs commands five times), the sooner you become debt-free!

Pay Now, Play Later

Psychologists call this delayed gratification. The Bible calls this spiritual maturity. Unfortunately, Ruthie and I did the exact opposite—and after 10 years of marriage, we had nothing to show for it except a lot of debt. We had some friends, however, who decided to pay the price to get out of debt and stay out of debt. After 10 years of marriage, they had $500,000 in the bank. What makes this even more remarkable is that they did this on their salaries as a policeman and a school teacher. "How did they do it?" you may ask. They each earned approximately $30,000 per year. They decided to live off one salary and invest the other. So they invested $30,000 per year in mutual funds (in the 1990s when such investments were performing well) for 10 years. When they were 32, they woke up one morning and had $500,000.

They simply chose to pay the price to get ahead early in their marriage. And now they're enjoying the fruits of their sacrifice. They have options. For example, the wife had a baby, and she decided she wanted to stay home with their newborn. She did it without any financial problems; after all, they were already used to living on only the husband's salary. While some women prefer to continue working after having children, she was pleased to have the option to stay home.

Some of the best wisdom I know for two-income families is to figure out a way to live on one salary. Getting tied to both incomes is a trap that many later wish they could escape. The benefits are great—you can save, invest, pay off debt, or do something else with the second salary.

chapter **6**

Be Disciplined in Your Efforts (Part 2)

Pay Attention to those Pennies

One day as I was walking, I found a penny. I didn't pick it up. I intentionally left it there. After all, a penny is not worth anything. A few steps beyond the penny, God compelled me to "turn around, pick up the penny, and apply it to your debt." I responded, "You've got to be kidding!" He wasn't kidding. I retrieved the penny and treated it like it was worth a million dollars. I deposited it in the bank and added it to our debt-elimination snowball.

Soon thereafter, I found a nickel. God responded with the same message. I obeyed. Shortly thereafter, I found a dime, then a quarter. I continued to apply all found money toward debt. Next, I received a $100 bill in the mailbox. It had been mailed anonymously. Though God likely used a human being to send that money, he may have done it himself. Did you know that God has envelopes? Did you know that God has stamps? Did you know God has money? Let's assume for a moment that God couldn't find a human who was willing to listen to his command to send a $100 bill to me in the mail. That wouldn't stop God from doing anything he pleased! The Bible assures us that if God cannot find a human to sing praises to his name, he can make the rocks cry out praises to him!

> Use every penny available to fight debt — even those you find on the street!

A short time later, God brought us $1000 in surprise money. Then, he brought us $5000 in surprise money. I could hardly wait to see what was next!

One day I read in Matthew 25:21, "The Master answered, 'You are a good servant who can be trusted. You proved yourself faithful with the small things. I can now make you the ruler of much greater things.'" I believe God's response to me was, "You showed yourself faithful with the pennies; I can trust you with more."

By paying attention to the pennies, you prove yourself trustworthy to God. You also sensitize yourself to small amounts of money. One of these benefits is supernatural, and the other is psychological. Added together, these produce powerful debt-reducing results.

While I was leading the "Conquering Debt God's Way" seminar in a local church, a pastor approached me during a break. He explained that he was formerly on the staff of a church that had 1000 known millionaires. After rubbing shoulders with them for several years, he shared with me a theme that was consistently communicated by them: "I didn't become a millionaire by paying attention to the dollars. I became a millionaire by paying attention to the pennies!"

Cut Up All Credit Cards

Close all of your credit accounts. Your creditors will still consider your account active unless you specifically request that they close your account, even if you haven't used the account in a long time. While I see no inherent evil in credit cards themselves, they're an entirely too convenient method of payment for most of us. This ease of spending helps credit cards bring many people down before they even know what happened. Some estimate

that many of us will spend 30% more when using credit
cards than we would spend with
cash or checks—even if we pay
the card off each month.

Spending is easier with a credit card — so get rid of it!

Some ask the question, "Shouldn't I keep the credit card
for emergencies?" I say, "No." Let's trust God with our emergencies. In fact, I believe that many people have poor prayer
lives as a result of having credit cards. After all, who needs
God during a time of emergency when we have a credit card
in our pocket to handle the emergency?

Further, credit cards themselves have put many of us in
a literal month-to-month emergency. Why hold onto the
very thing that's causing us so much debt strain? Doing so
is like telling an alcoholic who wants to break his addiction to get rid of all the alcohol in his house—except for
one bottle of vodka, just in case there's an emergency. It
simply doesn't make sense.

If you insist on keeping a credit card, I recommend
you live without one for at least six months. Then get one.
That hiatus will give you the opportunity to break any
dependency you may have, and you can discover that true
and abundant life in Christ can be experienced without
a credit card.

Quit Your Addictions

Even seemingly harmless addictions can put a huge strain
on your budget. Instead of continuing to be a slave to them,
quit them and put the savings in your monthly snowball. I
have a friend who used to drink 6 liters of Diet Coke™ per
day, which cost him $296 per month. After attending the
seminar, he sensed God leading him to limit his consump-
tion of Diet Coke™ to one can per day. This freed up over
$275 per month for him to put toward debt-elimination.

Others have stopped addictive behaviors, such as smoking and overeating, in order to accelerate their debt payoff while simultaneously improving their health. A great idea! Let me share with you how to cut your grocery bill in half (for adults only). Buy half the food you're used to buying; prepare half the food you're used to preparing; and eat half the food you're used to eating! If you're an average American, this won't kill you; in fact, it may actually help you. A recent study (*National Geographic*, November 1997, among many others) revealed that the one thing that researchers know for certain is that by eating less food, we can live longer and healthier lives. This shouldn't surprise us, as we're warned many times in God's Word to refrain from gluttony. I call this buy-half-prepare-half-eat-half diet the "Conquering Debt God's Way" diet. People all over are losing weight on it — while freeing up hundreds of dollars for debt-elimination.

Never Compromise Your Integrity!

There are some things in life that are more important than becoming debt-free. One of those things is maintaining your integrity.

In my organizer, I've written out a life mission statement that includes the phrase "always pay the green fees." For me this phrase stands for integrity. A few years ago, I played golf on a course that was closed. No one was there to accept my green fee. I could have played for free and no one would have ever known. However, when I got home, I sent a note to the golf course manager explaining what had happened, enclosing a check for the estimated green fee. We must remain committed to integrity.

My hope and prayer is that those who know me the best will respect me the most. It's easy to impress a crowd from a distance. But what do those closest to me think about me? Living a life of integrity leads to being respected — even by those who know the real you. Compromising integrity leads to a lack of respect from those who know the real you. We must be people committed to integrity.

You'll be given opportunities to get out of debt faster if you'll only compromise your integrity. You may see the opportunity to compromise in one area and the temptation will be to cheat so you can reduce debt

"Better is the poor who walks in his integrity than he who is crooked though he be rich."

Proverbs 28:6

faster. However, don't do it — it's never worth it!

Commit to a 30-Day Extra Purchase Wait List

Our plan hasn't shown much flexibility to this point. It now becomes flexible. In fact, a danger lies in sabotaging the entire plan simply by abusing this principle. Please take care not to go too far with it.

For determining when to make extra purchases, we suggest you use the "stoplight" method. There will be times when you need something that isn't in your budget. The question becomes, "May I meet this need with my snowball?" The answer is two-fold:

First, don't make a habit of using your snowball for non-debt reduction purposes or you'll never get out of debt.

Second, write the need down on a piece of paper and date it. Then pray about it for 30 days. If the Lord gives you (and your spouse if you're married) a "green light" — "the peace that passeth understanding" — then make the purchase without guilt. However, if either spouse has a red or yellow light (a hesitation in your heart, or a clear "no" from the Lord), then don't make the purchase.

I feel the need to address an issue at this point. Many men make one of two hurtful mistakes in marriage. They either say, "Here honey, take care of the finances," and they fail to take any responsibility for them, or they say, "Honey, you take care of the domestic duties, and I'll take care of the finances." The first mistake puts a very unfair burden on the wife. The second mistake communicates that the wife's opinion isn't worth much. Either scenario is harmful. Ruthie and I work as a team. We have joint bank accounts, pay bills together, pray together, and obey God together. We're soul-mates who love each other and practice mutual submission together (Ephesians 5:21). We are friends, partners, and comrades.

Now before you make a judgement about who "wears the pants" in our family, let me share with you the attitude of my wife. Ruthie long ago committed herself to be submissive to me (Ephesians 5:22) and has followed my loving leadership (Ephesians 5:25) for years. She's been willing to move, change jobs, and many other things, simply based on my conviction that God was leading us in that direction. However, I've learned (the hard way) that God often speaks to me through my wife (and vice versa). Therefore, I don't make major decisions until my wife and I have agreement in our hearts under God about it. After all, the Holy Spirit who gives me the "peace that passeth understanding" is the same Holy Spirit who gives her the "peace that passeth understanding." If we don't both get a "green light" from God, we don't do anything at that time.

Please don't use this "stoplight" principle as a club with which to beat your spouse. There may be times when you're tempted to get back at your spouse for something, so you intentionally say "No, we can't do that—because I don't have a green light about it." That response is totally inappropriate.

Record Every Penny in a Spending Log

If you have a problem with your weight, many weight loss clinics ask you to keep an "eating log." They suggest that you write down everything you eat so you can see the truth, evaluate it, and develop a strategy for change. If you have a problem with time management, many experts ask you to keep a "time log." They suggest that you write down how you spend your time so you can see the truth, evaluate it, and develop a strategy for change.

Keeping a spending log is the only way we're aware of to track down and slay the Miscellaneous Monster. As we've already said, the Miscellaneous Monster is invisible, yet very real. He sneaks up on your money and gobbles it up in the most mysterious of ways. How many times have you had money seem to disappear, only to realize that you have no idea where it went? This is the Miscellaneous Monster at work.

Keeping a spending log is very simple and is worth so much. It can, in effect, earn many people from $500 to $1,000 per hour. Why? Because average Americans lose 15% to 30% of their income to the Miscellaneous Monster — the equivalent of $6,000 to $12,000

> The average American loses 15–30% of income to the Miscellaneous Monster.

per year for those with a $40,000 per year income. By spending only 2 minutes per day, you can discover the truth about where your money is going, evaluate it, and change the way you spend it, freeing up thousands for debt-elimination.

Take Responsibility for Your Financial Future

In Genesis, we find Adam and Eve eating the forbidden fruit. When God asked Adam what had taken place, he blamed Eve. When he asked Eve what had happened, she blamed the serpent. We've been a society of blamers ever since. We blame our parents, our grandparents, our bosses, our environment, and the economy for all our problems. Generally, however, our biggest problems are ourselves. Most of us are where we are financially today because of decisions we made yesterday. Let's quit making excuses and stop blaming and simply face the fact: we're most likely the cause of our financial trouble.

We don't take lightly the reality that some are in the financial condition they are in because they were victims of a terrible accident or an awful disease. My heart goes out to all who find themselves in these circumstances. However, for most of us, it's been a matter of unwise choices — not victimization.

Realize also that everybody on the globe has a financial agenda for you. Banks, auto dealerships, insurance agents, and department stores all want to tell you what to do with your money. It's your job to tune out all the messages from the world and to tune in God's financial agenda. The choice is yours. Positive and negative consequences await you, depending on which agenda you choose.

Do It Yourself!

Your house may need cleaning —
  but you don't have to hire it done.
Your car may need washing —
  but you don't have to hire it done.
Your oil may need changing —
  but you don't have to hire it done.
Your body may need food —
  but you don't have to eat out.

We'll never forget when a lady came to us in tears and said, "Thank you for saving my life." We asked her what she meant and she proceeded to say, "I was planning on ending my life, but this seminar has helped me to see that there's hope. There's light at the end of the tunnel." She went on to say how God had awakened her in the middle of the night and instructed her to remove her false fingernails. This was no small issue for this lady. She was obsessed with beautiful fingernails. She became convinced that she should do her own nails while she was at war with debt and was willing to make that "sacrifice" even though her nails wouldn't look as good. She understood that she could not live life as she always had and get out of debt. She made some painful, yet rewarding, changes.

Consider Converting Your Insurance

We presently have term life insurance, with $500,000 of coverage on Bruce to allow Ruthie to stay at home and rear our daughters as she does now, $75,000 on Ruthie to cover burial costs and pay off any debt, and $5,000 on each of our daughters. If both spouses work full-time, your insurance coverage would have a different husband/wife coverage ratio than ours. We receive all this coverage for $58 per month.

A friend of ours had a cash value policy with $250,000 on himself, and it cost him $230 per month. He decided to convert his cash value policy to term and to put the difference in his

> Converting cash life insurance to term life insurance may give you extra money to fight debt...

monthly snowball. He even decided to cash in the cash portion of the policy and put it toward his debt.

While there are some important ramifications for converting to term life insurance, it may be a good option in your battle with debt. If you do decide to do this, you'll want to have the new policy in force before you cancel the old one in order to protect you from discovering a serious health condition or even dying "between policies!" This may not make sense for everyone, but it's worth considering.

Reward Yourself

On occasion, reward yourself for work well done. Be careful—don't get carried away with this or you'll never become debt-free. We recommend using the "stoplight" method described above in determining what to do; it works best when you determine a reward schedule *in advance*. Don't get into the habit of impulsively rewarding yourself. Impulsive spending is an enemy to debt-free living.

Here's a recommended reward guideline:

> On the day when you pay off your #1 debt, eat out at a nice restaurant;

> On the day when you pay off all but your mortgage, use half of your monthly snowball to do something fun (one time only!);

> On the day when you're finally debt-free, use your entire monthly snowball to celebrate (one time only!).

Invent Your Own Ways to Attack Debt

Be creative! We changed to a bank that had no service charge, saving us $10 per month. Of course, we added the money to our snowball.

We ran across a "golf mat" that I had received as a gift more than a year before. It was unused and still in its original box. A local golf store was happy to give us money back for it.

Some friends of ours found a Kenmore™ icemaker that had been given to them as a wedding gift 10 years earlier. It was still in the original box and unopened. They took it back to Sears and received a refund, which they promptly applied to their debt.

Another friend of ours used to eat out for lunch 20 days a month at $5 per day. He discovered that he could pack a sack lunch for less than $1 per day, freeing up over $80 per month for debt elimination.

I stopped working out at the "XYZ" Club at $30 per month and began working out at the "ABC" Club for $15 per month. We immediately added the savings to debt elimination.

A long distance phone company told us they would send us a check for $75 simply for trying them out. We did—and put the $75 toward debt!

Some people have cancelled magazine subscriptions before they expire and requested a refund for the remaining issues.

In short, there are many other exciting strategies for you to apply to your debt-reduction plans—and they're just waiting for you to discover them. Be creative, and you may even have fun finding new ways to attack debt!

Well, that just about does it for the "Conquering Debt God's Way" system. The techniques and tips we've outlined in the past few chapters have helped many people in the fight to reduce debt, but there's one more thing you have to do if you really want to *conquer* it. Now it's time for you to see the big picture by looking at this final step—the briefest, but by far the most important part of the system.

chapter **7**

Look to God for Divine Intervention

As I said, this is the shortest, but most powerful and important part of the "Conquering Debt God's Way" plan. Why is it so powerful? Because this part of the plan is all about God. Why is it so brief? Because this part of the plan is all about God and his miraculous intervention—and no amount of explanation or discussion will change one important fact: he wants to help you!

In Joshua 10:11–14, the Bible says,

As they fled before Israel on the road down from Beth Horon to Azekah, the Lord hurled large hailstones down on them from the sky, and more of them died from the hailstones than were killed by the swords of the Israelites. On the day the Lord gave the Amorites over to Israel, Joshua said to the Lord in the presence of Israel: 'O sun, stand still over Gibeon, O moon over the Valley of Aijalon.' So the sun stood still, and the moon stopped, till the nation avenged itself on its enemies, as is written in the Book of Jashar. The sun stopped in the middle of the sky and delayed going down about a full day... Surely the Lord was fighting for Israel!

We see God here miraculously helping his children to conquer the enemy that he had commanded them to conquer. How would you like God to help you to conquer your enemy—debt?

God wants to help you! The Bible reveals that God is concerned about our financial debt. And God often did financial miracles to enable people to experience miraculous debt elimination. In 1 Samuel 17, God miraculously canceled the debt of David's father. In Nehemiah 5, God miraculously canceled the debts of Nehemiah's workmen. In 2 Kings 4, it was the widow's debt. In Matthew 17, it was Jesus' and Peter's debt. In Philemon 18 and 19, it was Onesimus' debt.

God is still doing this today. My family has personally experienced this grace, as have thousands of others who have applied these principles.

There are some prerequisites to experiencing God's miraculous intervention. First, you need to have taken the other steps of the "Conquering Debt God's Way" process before looking to God for miracles. Second, don't expect God's help if you're unwilling to become committed — to tithe, to give offerings, to sell stuff, or to make any of the other sacrifices to which God may call you.

The Bible makes it clear. Joshua didn't withdraw to a shade tree with a soft drink and expect God to finish the job for him. Joshua continued to do battle with the sword, while dependently leaning upon God for help. This biblical example depicts a beautiful picture, which I attempted to represent accurately in the "Vow to Declare War on Debt" (page 133): "Whether by miracle or our own dogged determination, we vow to be debt-free." This vow states a dependency on God while simultaneously communicating our personal commitment to the task.

The application of this step is as simple as ABC.

> **A**sk God for help. The Bible says God likes us to ask him for help. God loves it when we acknowledge our need of him. In what I believe to be the greatest prayer promise in all of Scripture (1 John 5:14–16), we are taught that there are two prerequisites to answered prayer: the first is simply that we ask! The Bible also teaches that we don't have because we don't ask. I don't know about you, but I don't want to be missing things because I haven't asked.

Of course, the Bible also says that we sometimes lack things because we've asked improperly; I would never encourage anyone to ask intentionally for the wrong reasons. However, we often don't know if we're asking improperly or not. In these instances, I think we should ask just in case.

> **B**elieve that God will help. The Bible teaches that "without faith, it is impossible to please God." God is pleased when we really believe. After asking God for help, Ruthie and I communicated to God, "We really believe you will help us. We literally expect miracles. We don't know how or when, but we look forward to seeing your supernatural involvement in our debt-elimination journey."

> | **The ABCs of God's Intervention** | |
> | --- | --- |
> | **A**sk God to help you. | |
> | **B**elieve that God will help you. | |
> | **C**ontinue paying off debt with a passion! | |

> **C**ontinue attacking debt with a passion — regardless of what God does or does not do. God always knows what's best. He may want to develop character qualities in you that will be truly valuable to you and his kingdom. He may choose to develop these qualities through training in perseverance rather than by miraculous debt elimination. Whether God performs a miracle or not, keep on demonstrating to yourself and to him that you're committed to the task to which he has called you.

Work at conquering debt God's way as if success is entirely dependent upon you. On the other hand, pray, trust, and believe as if your success is entirely dependent upon God! If you do this, you can conquer debt — God's way.

chapter **8**

Questions and Answers

Q: I only have a house and car payment. How do I come up with a snowball?

A: Ironically, those who have been the most financially responsible have the least potential when it comes to a snowball. Those who have the most debt have the most snowball potential. Don't be discouraged. Due to your financial responsibility, you really do not need a snowball as badly as those who have blown it big time.

However, rapid debt elimination is still a wonderful goal for you. My recommendation is to spend less, sell stuff, make more, and ask God for a miracle. These things still enable you to create a debt-elimination snowball.

I gave this simple answer to a family who called me several years ago. Within 3 years, they informed me that they had paid off their house and car and were completely debt-free. Be encouraged. Total debt elimination is still reachable, even without a long list of 15 debts from which to create a snowball.

Q: After applying the Quick Cash Flow Creation Formula to my debts, I find myself discouraged as my #1 target is 18 months from being paid off. Any advice?

A: You must find a way to knock that first debt off quickly. This generates excitement and gets the snowball rolling. If you don't see success before 18 months, it's too easy to give up. Aggressively cut back expenses, sell stuff, take extra jobs, etc. You know the drill! Just realize that these actions are more important for you than those whose first debt target is only three months away.

Q: How can I buy Christmas gifts without a credit card?

A: Do you remember spending plan Bank Account #2 described on pages 83–88 (and in the worksheet on page 149)? We put $50 each month in this account for Christmas gifts, enabling our family to withdraw $600 in cash each year.

This $600 must cover gifts for one grandparent, our parents (4), our children (3), each other (2), our siblings and their spouses (12), and nieces and nephews (15).

If this sounds impossible, it's because it nearly is. We do it by actually buying gifts for our grandparents and parents, each other, and our children. Then we draw names among our siblings, so Ruthie and I only buy one gift each at the sibling level. Our children and their cousins also draw names, resulting in our three daughters purchasing only one gift each.

Additionally, it's a great idea to agree among family members that all gifts must be made by your own hands. This saves money, and also increases the sentimental value of the gifts.

You may even want to cut back on the number of gifts you get your children. My sister Shanda will not buy more than three gifts for each of her children. The reason: Jesus only received three gifts at his birth. It doesn't seem right to her to get her children more than three—a point that's worth thinking about.

You may need to also cut back on the amount of money you spend on each gift. Though this may be a difficult transition for your children to make, it won't kill them. Take them aside before Christmas and explain that God is leading your family to make some sacrifices in order to become debt-free. Let them know exactly what this commitment means. It is good for your children to see you follow God's will for your lives even when it involves sacrifice. Please model personal sacrifice if you are requiring your children to sacrifice. It would be unhealthy for your children to see their parents exchanging expensive gifts when their personal Christmas is cut to the bone. In addition, we have minimized the emphasis on big gift purchasing for one another. After all, we are commemorating Jesus' birthday, not ours.

Our family also gives a Christmas gift to Jesus. We believe its value should be more than the value of the most expensive gift we give to anyone else. For example, if the most I spend on any gift is $67 (for my wife), I believe I should give at least $68 to Jesus. This gift is given above our tithe and offerings. We give this money to special projects at our church or to Kingdom-building, para-church ministries.

Q: Should I tithe out of my contributions to my retirement plan?

A: It's my opinion that if you sign a salary reduction agreement so a portion of your salary can be sent to a 401(k) or similar retirement plan, you've literally reduced your salary. You'd therefore tithe on the reduced salary amount. When you withdraw your retirement contributions, then you'll pay tithe on the amount you've withdrawn.

Q: Should I tithe out of company benefits?

A: Again, this is my opinion. I'm not sure I'm correct, but the following makes sense to me. I don't believe you should tithe on designated money. For example, some relatives gave us some money for the purpose of buying a new refrigerator. They were very clear with us. We were to use the money to buy a refrigerator and nothing else. We didn't tithe on that money because we used all of it to buy a new refrigerator. I believe we made the right decision. Think of this another way. If you give $100 to your church and designate it to the youth fund, what should your church do with it? They should put it towards the youth fund. Anything else would be unethical. I believe this same principle applies to company benefits, too. I'm referring to company benefits that are automatically yours because you work there; you don't have the option of doing without these benefits and receiving the money. You aren't given the option of receiving cash instead. Though these benefits have a definite financial value and are certainly a blessing, they're designated and therefore do not fall under the category of income which should be tithed. I would encourage you to pray about this to seek the peace of the Lord about what you should do.

Q: How do I go about purchasing automobiles without going into debt?

A: While I believe that we should be able to pay cash for automobiles someday, it's unrealistic to eliminate debt aggressively while saving money in a car replacement fund simultaneously. Therefore, we chose to attack debt aggressively and to ignore future vehicle needs temporarily. After all our debt was eliminated, we decided to use a portion of our snowball to start a vehicle replacement fund.

You encounter another problem if you need a car before you get all your debt paid off. Here's what we did when we encountered such a problem: we refused to listen to the wisdom of this world, which says "buy all the car you can for the least payment amount possible."

This is how many people buy a car, using what's commonly called a lease. A lease allows you to "rent" more car than you'd be able to afford at your income level. Of course, leasing a car instead of buying it is like renting a house instead of buying. While this may make sense occasionally, it's often much wiser to purchase. Leasing is a trap that's difficult to break, because at the end of the lease, you'll still need a car, but you won't own one, so you'll have nothing to trade in. Since it's quite easy to exceed the maximum allowable miles, you'll often face an extra miles penalty—which the dealer will usually offer to waive provided you enter into another lease. With no money to pay the penalty and no trade-in to use as a down payment, signing another lease may seem to be the only solution—not to mention the lure of driving a brand-new automobile! It's easy to get permanently stuck in this cycle.

Ruthie and I decided once again to reverse the wisdom of this world. First, we made sure we really needed another car. We try to drive cars until they're 12 years old or older. We drive them well over 150,000 miles if at all possible. Even expensive repairs are not usually as costly as monthly payments. After determining that we really needed a car, we decided to buy the least expensive car that met our needs and to put the largest monthly payment possible toward it. At this point, our snowball was $750 per month. We borrowed for the car (a 9-year-old Honda Accord with 87,000 miles—$5500), took a reprieve from adding to our house payment, and used the snowball to pay off the car in approximately eight months. Then we had a dependable, paid-off car, and resumed attacking the house payment with the snowball. Whatever you do, don't buy an automobile impulsively. Give God some time. He may choose to provide a car for you in another way. We've been the recipients of several automobiles as free gifts. Had we hurriedly made an impulsive purchase, God wouldn't have provided the miracle car.

Q: How do we purchase our dream home?

A: There are several ways to accomplish this goal. First, let God help you define your dream home. While God wants us to enjoy the riches he brings into our lives (1 Timothy 6:17b), he doesn't want us to live greedy, self-obsessed lives. Our dream home should be reasonable, even if we have unlimited income. Buying a house to "keep up with the Joneses" is tempting, but inappropriate for the Christian. However, having a nice home for min-istry purposes or entertaining may make sense. One way to make this purchase is first to buy *half* the house you qualify for and second, to *double* the monthly payment. This enables you to pay off your initial house in approxi-mately five years. Third, save the monthly payment until it can be added to the sale of the first home and pay cash for your dream home. Once the first home is paid for, another possibility is to turn it into a rental property, borrowing money for your dream home while your first home provides rental income for you. In addition, you could sell the dream home and move into the rental if you experience a financial setback. Many other varia-tions are acceptable. Use your creativity—and pray!

Q: Should I follow the "buy half the house and double the payment" strategy if it would require me to live in an unsafe area?

A: There are more important things in life than paying off a house in 5 years. I would never recommend that you buy a house in an unsafe neighborhood. I'd also not recommend buying a house that would be impossible to resell. Therefore, while buying less house than you qualify for is often wise, you may not be able to buy a house wisely that's 50% below what you qualify for.

Q: Should I sell my house and buy down?

A: While that's a legitimate debt-reduction strategy, it's often unnecessary. Pray about your options and look for harmony between you and your spouse before making such a drastic move. Also, run the numbers carefully. After paying real estate agent fees, closing costs, and moving expenses, downsizing may not always pay as much as you'd imagine or wish.

Q: Is it important to set a lifestyle and stick with it?

A: I recently ran into a gentleman who sold a business he had developed—for an unbelievable profit. He had more money than he knew what to do with. His first response was to buy new cars, a new house, etc. As he continued to prosper, he continued in this pattern for quite some time. Then, it dawned on him: it was simply not appropriate to continue to buy bigger and better houses the rest of his life. At some point, his house (like all his other possessions) was more than adequate. Even though he had the money to continue to upgrade his lifestyle, he *voluntarily* chose to limit his lifestyle and to become a hilarious and generous giver to the kingdom of God. If you're gifted in making money, realize that God's purpose in gifting you this way is not so you can spoil yourself. God has gifted you to produce large sums of money so you can *give* large sums of money. I don't know that there is a clear lifestyle line that should be drawn for everybody. Instead, prayerfully ask God to reveal his lifestyle plan for you. Then follow his plan with generosity and without guilt. My wife Ruthie recently shared this principle with me as she said: "There comes a point when you have enough shoes. You have enough clothes. Your kids have enough clothes." God will speak to you about these things if you will only pursue him and his direction.

Q: What are the most common mistakes people make?

A: After experiencing some success, the urgency of debt elimination often disappears. When you're $200 per month short of meeting expenses, you have to eliminate debt aggressively in order to survive. But when you have an extra $500 per month, it's easy to lose the focus and get lazy. This can result in turning the debt-eliminating snowball into living expenses for an excessive lifestyle upgrade, or even using it to go further into debt. Failure to follow through and pay off all debt is also possible.

Q: How do I implement these principles without devastating our teenagers, who happen to be a little bit spoiled?

A: A better question might be: is God calling you to conquer debt God's way? If so, he wants your teens to go through this with you, and he'll provide them the grace to get through it. Remember: you must communicate with them and be a consistent model for them.

Q: How can I affordably feed my family?

A: Follow these simple steps:

   1] Make a menu that includes healthy meals the family likes without being extravagant. Include snacks if needed;
   2] List all the ingredients you need for the menu;
   3] Determine which ingredients you already have on hand and cross them off the list;

4] Purchase only remaining ingredients on list.

Be aware of "wants vs. needs" so you can minimize grocery costs.

Q: My spouse and I never agree on big issues. Now we're even arguing over which conquering debt strategies to implement. Any suggestions?

A: Some things in life are more important than aggressive debt elimination. One of those things is marital harmony. When confronted with major decisions, Ruthie and I pray for approximately thirty days. After this season of prayer, we compare the convictions we have in our hearts. What we're looking for is the peace of the Lord ruling in our hearts. We even did this regarding our decision to publish this book! If we both have the peace of God, we proceed. If either of us has a hesitancy in our hearts, we don't proceed. I'm convinced that God often speaks to us through our spouses. Assuming that we are where we are today because of the Lord's leadership, we don't want to make a major change unless God directs us to. If we worship the same God (which we do), then his will is the same for both of us. He is perfectly capable of giving both spouses peace about anything he leads us to do.

Q: Is it a sin to use a credit card?

A: Ruthie and I lived for about a year without a credit card. We didn't do without one because we thought it was a sin to use a credit card—I don't believe that it is. We did so because we needed to break our terrible credit card habits. After we learned to live without credit cards, we got one once again. We seldom use it and are very responsible with it when we do.

Q: Does it ever make sense to go into debt?

A: The Bible doesn't prohibit debt. I believe that this is because it sometimes makes sense to go into debt. I've heard it said that it makes sense to borrow for appreciating items and it makes no sense to borrow for depreciating items. This sounds wise to me. If we were to limit ourselves by this principle, home purchases and college education would be about the only items for which we might borrow. Another example might be to purchase a business (you might also consider my response above about purchasing automobiles without going into debt). Finally, make sure you go into debt neither quickly nor impulsively. God may have another plan to meet your need. Give him some time. In addition, pray before going into debt for any reason. If you (and your spouse, if you're married) don't have the peace of God ruling in your heart, don't go into debt.

chapter **9**

Concluding Thoughts

Thus far, I've taken about 3 hours of your time (estimated reading time) to tell you what I could have told you in 3 minutes. "Why would you do that?" you ask? Because I'm a preacher! We specialize in taking 3 minutes' worth of material and turning it into 3 hours of information. Then we break it down into 30-minute segments and call it a 6-week sermon series!

Here's the entire system in 3 minutes:

1] *Define your enemy.* You must be personally convinced that debt is your enemy; it's not your friend. I have illustrated this by discussing your mortgage, automobile loans, the reality of 96% credit card debt, the effects of long-term debt upon your health and family, and the neglecting of the Great Commission.

2] *Declare war against your enemy.* You must become radically committed and focused to defeat debt. It takes a warlike commitment. Sign the "Vow to Declare War on Debt" (page 133), mean it, and give a copy to your pastor, preacher, or elder as a public expression of your commitment to God.

3] *Demonstrate fearless faith.* Once you hear God, obey him—whether his message makes sense to your human, finite mind or not. Commit to God the top of your income, enlisting his supernatural involvement in your finances. Sign the "Vow to Demonstrate Fearless Faith" (page 135), mean it, and give a copy to your pastor, preacher, or elder as a public expression of your commitment to God.

4] *Be disciplined in your efforts.* Follow the Snowball Payoff Priority Plan, sell stuff, minimize all living expenses, don't compromise your budget, sell more stuff, temporarily discontinue retirement savings, consider using accumulated savings, take extra jobs, sell more stuff, stand firm against magic pill solutions, commit to pay now and play later, add salary raises and bonuses to your debt-reduction snowball, sell more stuff, add IRS refunds and surprise money to your snowball, pay attention to the pennies, etc. In short, radically attack debt in a disciplined fashion with every penny you can get your hands on.

5] *Ask God for divine intervention.* Ask God for a miracle. Believe he will supernaturally help you. And continue attacking debt with a passion whether God intervenes or not.

You may want to review this summary every week for awhile. This renewing of your mind will help to transform you (Romans 12:1).

While Joshua is one of my all-time Bible heroes, and while he demonstrated obedience about as well as any other Bible character, he was still a sinful human. He made a crucial mistake that came back to haunt the children of God many years later. In Joshua 11:22, we read, "there were no Amorites left in the land of the sons of Israel. Only in Gaza, in Gath, and in Ashdod, some remained."

Why would God have included such a verse in his Word? To teach us a valuable lesson. God's command to Joshua was to eliminate all of the Amorites, not just most of the Anakim. My friend and former Pastor, Dr. Charles Murray, said it best: "Incomplete obedience is disobedience." While Joshua was highly obedient, he failed to obey by finishing the job completely. The moral to the story of Joshua is that when God gives you a task, you must be sure to complete it.

I personally believe that in most cases, God wants us to be completely debt-free, including house and cars. The temptation is to get *most* of the debt paid off, and then to relax and let a portion of one's debt survive. I've heard it stated this way: "If I can just get my credit cards paid off, I'll be satisfied. Besides, I've always believed that everybody will always have a house payment and a car payment." This attitude can lead you to relax far too early. And this leaves the door open for your remaining debt to come back and haunt you in the future.

I was asked once, "Why should I pay off my house, which only charges me 8% interest, when I can earn 15% through investing in mutual funds?" Several answers come to mind. First, when you pay extra money toward a house, you're guaranteed results of 8%. At the time of this writing, the stock market is doing some most interesting things. Though it has set some records for gains in recent years, it has also set records in the loss column. It's just as possible to lose 15% on your money invested as it is to gain 15%. This leads me to think house payoff is a good idea.

Another gentleman asked, "Why should I pay off my house? It's the last good tax deduction I have left." There's actually a better tax deduction available than the mortgage interest write-off—it's called charitable giving. If you're really looking for a great tax write-off, it often makes sense to pay off the house quickly, and then give away your entire house payment amount each month to your local church or other deserving ministry or charity. This results in getting to take 100% as a tax deduction instead of only the interest portion. In addition, you're now using this money for ministry purposes in the kingdom of God instead of throwing it away in the form of interest.

Though this information is accurate as of the date of this writing, it may not apply to everyone. The IRS limits the charitable giving that is tax deductible. Most of the population will not likely need to worry about exceeding this amount, but those who make substantial income could. Please consult your CPA for specifics in the ever-changing tax laws.

For those of you who discover that due to your income level, the charitable giving parameters exclude you from the tax deduction you want, consider the reality of this so-called tax benefit. Why would anyone throw away 75¢ on the dollar in interest in order to get a 25¢ tax break? Is this really a good deal? I think not! You'd actually be better off financially to go ahead and pay the additional 25¢ on each dollar earned and put the remaining 75¢ per dollar you earn in your pocket.

If none of this makes sense to you and you insist on having a house payment, it still seems wise to me to have a paid-off house somewhere. If the economy were to crash, as Larry Burkett predicts, you'll still need a house! If the economy indeed crashes, you could always move to the paid-for house. If it doesn't, you can make it rental property.

One man shared his story of turning debt into a fabulous income. He had mastered the art of borrowing money to purchase rental properties. He would then let his tenants pay off the loans for him through their monthly rent. He asked my opinion. While I recommended that he have a paid-off house somewhere in case of an emergency, I have no problem with what he's doing.

As we've noted several times, the Bible doesn't prohibit debt. Again, I'm convinced that this is because there are a few occasions (though a very few) when debt actually makes sense. The man mentioned in the previous paragraph was highly successful in what he was doing, and he was very generous with the kingdom of God and the needy. I agreed that what he was doing seemed to be God's will in his life.

Others have said that secured debt is not debt at all (unless you owe more on the loan than the value of the collateral) since you could sell the item to pay off the debt if needed. Maybe they're right. One thing I know for sure is that I don't have all the answers. In fact, I still make financial mistakes to this day (though far fewer than I used to). It just seems certain to me that complete debt elimination is wise. This brings a number of benefits: a healthy sense of security, no presumption upon the future, a daily experience of God's provision, options such as trading in the job you hate for a job you love (which pays less, but who cares—you don't need as big a salary if your house is paid off!) or the option of a working mother staying home with her children, and a place to live even if the economy does crash!

May God continue to bless you as you conquer debt God's way!

appendix

Conquering Debt God's Way

On the following pages, you'll find a series of forms, tables, and worksheets which we hope will be useful to you in your effort to conquer debt God's way.

We'd like to encourage you not only to fill in and work with the things you find here, but also to make photocopies of them for your own use. Ruthie and I made several copies of the vows we signed, for example, so that we could post them around the house and at our places of work. Having these copies so that we could see them throughout the day helped to remind us exactly what we were doing and why — and more importantly, they helped to remind us that the Lord was supporting and sustaining us in our battle.

You may notice that throughout this section, the pages on the left side are blank. That's because these pages serve as the backs of the various forms and worksheets, and we wanted to encourage you to cut out and use these resources without losing any important content.

As we've said throughout this book, you're not likely to succeed in your battle against debt without a real commitment and without constantly reminding yourself what the stakes are in conquering debt. We hope that the information in this book and the forms and worksheets in this appendix will offer guidance and encouragement to you as you fight debt, as you show fearless faith, and as you trust in God's help and support in your battle!

Vow to Declare War on Debt

We, the undersigned, choose this day to declare war on debt by making a solemn vow to God regarding our future financial direction.

We do not take this vow lightly. We understand that, "It is better that you should not vow than that you should vow and not pay" (Ecclesiastes 5:5). Yet we choose to make the following vow in order to declare war on debt formally and publicly.

From this day forward, we resolve to:

> No longer accept just getting by from paycheck to paycheck;

> Make rapid debt elimination our primary financial objective;

> Commit ourselves without reservation to conquering debt God's way;

> Attack debt with a passion.

We will apply complete follow-through to every action that pertains to our circumstances. We commit all of our efforts to eliminating our debts.

We believe that God may choose to cancel our debts miraculously. However, we also realize that it took time for us to get into debt, and it will most likely take time for us to get out of debt. Regardless, whether by miracle or our own dogged determination, we vow to become free from the bondage of debt!

_____   _____
signature   date

_____   _____
signature   date

For a discussion of this vow, see pages 35–41.

Vow to Demonstrate Fearless Faith

We, the undersigned, make a solemn vow to obey God from this day forward in the area of tithing.

We understand that tithing is:

> Commanded by God (Leviticus 27:30);

> Commended by Jesus (Matthew 23:23);

> An opportunity to prove we really love God (John 14:15);

> Ten percent of our gross income (Malachi 3:10);

> First-fruit giving (Proverbs 3:9);

> A demonstration that God has first place in our lives (Deuteronomy 14:23);

> To be given to our place of worship with no strings attached (Malachi 3:8–10);

> An expression of our gratitude to God;

> An acknowledgement that everything we have was given to us by God (Deuteronomy 8:18);

> The biblical prescription for turning our hearts wholly to the Lord (Matthew 6:21);

> A habit—we'll tithe like clockwork whether we're present at our home congregation or absent.

We acknowledge that the intent of this vow is not to limit our giving; it simply forms the foundation for our giving. We will remain sensitive to the Holy Spirit's leading in the area of giving offerings above and beyond our tithe. By becoming faithful tithers, we are trusting by faith that God will provide for the needs of our family and help us in our war on debt.

We choose to make this vow obediently and expectantly!

_____   _____
signature   date

_____   _____
signature   date

For a discussion of this vow, see pages 43–62.

Debt List

Creditor	Balance	Minimum Payment	"Months Left"
Totals	=	=	

For instructions about using this worksheet, see pages 66–68.

The Snowball Payoff Priority Plan

Creditor	Balance	"Months Left"	Minimum Payment	Snowball Amount

For instructions about using this worksheet, see pages 66–68.

Spending Plan

Use this worksheet to begin your planning. Sample categories are listed on the next page to help you identify and organize your monthly expenses. Once you've completed this table, you can use the worksheets on pages 147–151 to organize your spending using the 3-account system described on pages 83–88.

Category	Amount
Total Expenses	**=**

(left vertical label: Monthly Expenses)

For instructions about using this worksheet, see pages 83–88.

Sample Spending Plan Categories

Category	Description
Allowance	Allowance money for children
Automobile	Repair and maintenance, but not gas or insurance
Banking	Processing fees, check printing, etc.
Childcare	Babysitting expenses, nursery school costs, etc.
Clothing	Work and casual clothes
Debt	All debt other than home and auto debt
Eating out	Eating out – including tips
Education	School expenses for children
Entertainment	Movies, video rentals, dates with spouses, etc.
Gifts	Gifts for Christmas, birthday, weddings, etc.
Groceries	Food costs
Housing	Rent or mortgage (including property taxes)
Insurance	Auto, life, health, and house (if not included with mortgage)
Medical	Expenses not covered by insurance
Miscellaneous	Expenses not covered by other categories
Offerings	Gifts to church and charities above your tithe
Pets	Food, veterinarian costs, pet boarding, etc.
Reserve	Short-term savings for non-recurring expenses
Retirement	Payments to IRA, 401(k), and other retirement savings
Taxes	Federal and state income taxes
Telephone	Phone expenses including mobile phone charges
Tithe	10% of gross income
Utilities	Gas, electricity, water, etc.
Vacation	Transportation, meals, lodging, etc.

For a discussion of this list, see pages 83–88.

Income & Expenses Worksheet

Use this table to record your income. Don't forget to include income from part-time jobs and other sources—anything that you can count on as a regular part of your income. Then, subtract your total expenses (from page 141) and "momentum money"—5% of your gross income which you'll use as a sacrificial margin to reduce your debt. The remainder is money you can add to your Snowball amount or use in other ways to conquer debt.

	Category	Amount
Income		
	Income Total	
	Less Expenses (from page 141)	–
	Momentum Money (5% of income)	–
	Total	=

For instructions about using this worksheet, see pages 83–88.

Spending Plan Worksheet: Bank Account 1

Category	Amount
Tithe	
Offerings	
Electricity	
Gas	
Phone	
Water	
Debts:	
Momentum money (5% of income)	
Bank Account 1 Subtotal	**=**

Utilities and Regular Monthly Expenses

For instructions about using this worksheet, see pages 83–88.

Spending Plan Worksheet: Bank Account 2

	Category	Amount
Insurance	Car	
	Life	
	Health	
Taxes	State	
	Federal	
Medical		
Gifts		
Auto		
Other	Reserve (for unforeseen expenses)	
	Bank Account 2 Subtotal	**=**

For instructions about using this worksheet, see pages 83–88.

Spending Plan Worksheet: "Cash Expenses Box"

Category	Amount
Groceries	
Clothes	
Miscellaneous	
Entertainment	
Eating out	
"Cash Expenses Box" Subtotal	**=**

Needs / *Wants*

For instructions about using this worksheet, see pages 83–88.

Conquering Debt
God's Way
Seminars

Would you like to share the *Conquering Debt God's Way* system with your church or organization? One great way to do so is to host a seminar. For more information, go to <www.conqueringdebt.com> or call (806) 780-7615 to request a free information packet.

If Bruce is unavailable, please leave the following information on his voicemail:

Your name

Your position or title

Name of your church or organization

Mailing address

Daytime & evening phone numbers

Now available on video!

Let Bruce and Ruthie Ammons teach your next Sunday School series! If you can't attend the seminar, the *Conquering Debt God's Way* video series is the next best thing. In this VHS-format series, learn how to whittle away your Spirit-crippling debt, to utilize the tried-and-true Snowball Payoff Priority Plan, to manage your money while increasing both your tithe and your savings, to expect God's miracle money—and to do it all God's Way!

The series consists of 6 sessions presented on 3 tapes:

Tape 1:   Session 1 · 42 minutes
             Session 2 · 20 minutes

Tape 2:   Session 3 · 40 minutes
             Session 4 · 64 minutes

Tape 3:   Session 5 · 53 minutes
             Session 6 · 60 minutes

For more information or to order the *Conquering Debt God's Way* video series, go to <www.conqueringdebt.com> or call (806) 780-7615.

Bruce Ammons received his education from Wayland Baptist University and Southwestern Seminary. While at Wayland, he played on the school's basketball and tennis teams. But more importantly, he met Ruthie, the love of his life (they've been married for 20 years)! He now travels full-time, teaching the *Conquering Debt God's Way* seminar in churches of various denominations. He presently leads 67 seminars each year. Bruce enjoys traveling with his family, reading, and participating in sports. He also enjoys taking his daughters on a "daddy-daughter date" each week.